Play Piano in a Flash!®
THE NEXT STEP

Moving Forward With A Creative Style Approach To Playing Piano or Keyboard

By
Bradley Sowash
&
Scott Houston

© 2006 Houston Enterprises Press
a division of Houston Enterprises, Inc.
6320 Rucker Road, Suite E, Indianapolis, IN 46220
All Rights Reserved   International Copyrights Secured   Printed in the USA

TABLE OF CONTENTS

About The Authors 4

How To Use This Book 5

Chapter 1 - How to Construct Chords 6
Stacking Thirds to Create Chords   6
Counting 1/2 Steps to Create Chords   10

Chapter 2 - Principal Chords, and Inversions........................12
Principal Chords   12
Seventh Chords   13
Putting Principal Chords to Work   14
Inversions   15
Slash Chords   16

Chapter 3 - Left Hand Patterns and Basslines 19
Broken Chords   19
Broken Chords in Common Time   20
Chord Tones Are Everywhere   24
Basslines   25
Creating a Bassline by Changing Inversions   26
Passing Note Bass   29

Chapter 4 - Embellishing the Melody................................30
EZ Bassline   33
Rhythmic Embellishment   36
Melodic Embellishment   38
Chord Tone Embellishment   39
Putting Embellishments Together   40

Chapter 5 - Adding Fills and Improvising 42
Fills   45
The Pentatonic Scale   46
Filling with Chord Tones   47
The Jazz Solo   49

Chapter 6 - Combining Melody, Harmony and Bass 54
The Elements of Music   54
Right Hand Combo   55
Open and Closed Broken Chords   60
Left Hand Combos   61
Broken Chords   62
Open and Closed Broken Chords in 4/4 Time   65
Stride   66
Faux Stride   66
Waltz   67
Faux Waltz   68

Chapter 7 - How Chords Function 69
Chord Function   69
Home Base - The I Chord   70
Third Base - The V7 Chord   71
Home Run - The V7 - I Cadence   72
Second Base - The IV Chord   73

Chapter 8 - Intros, Turnarounds and Endings 74

Introductions	74
The Master of Ceremonies V7 Chord	74
Time Stretch	75
Passing Note Bass	75
Hand Over Hand	75
Last Few Measures	76
Send in a Substitution	77
Combinations	77
Turnarounds	78
Substitute V7 Chord (Again)	79
The ii7 Chord	80
Second Base Substitution	81
First Base - The vi Chord	82
The Classic Turnaround	82
Transposing Turnarounds	84
Endings	85
Plagal Cadence - Amen!	87
Rock Whole Step Ending	88
Jazz Cadence - The Sideslip	89

Chapter 9 - Putting It All Together 91

Pick a song	91
Find a source	92
Creating a skeletal version	94
Pick a style	94
Work out the mechanics	94
Add in the extras	95
Put it all together	95

About The Authors

Bradley Sowash

An accomplished composer, educator, critically-acclaimed recording artist of seven CDs, and concert jazz pianist, Bradley Sowash has delighted listeners of all ages in concert halls and churches throughout the United States and Europe for over two decades. His emotional style and formidable technique have prompted favorable reviews in national publications including The Village Voice's comment that *"Sowash's music powerfully conjures the moods."* Known for his instant audience rapport, Billboard Magazine declared *"He can really move an audience along with zest and wit."* His music has received national airplay including on NPR's "Morning Edition" and he continues to be a regular guest on the Public Television series, "The Piano Guy." Other publications by Sowash include *That's Jazz,* a piano method published by the Neil A. Kjos Music Company, several volumes of jazz hymn arrangements published by Augsburg Fortress Press and numerous piano books for all ability levels published by Bradley Sowash Music. For more information visit www.bradleysowash.com

Scott Houston

Host and Co-Producer of the weekly television series, "The Piano Guy," Scott has entertained and educated literally millions of viewers with his simple message that playing piano should be fun. Recognizing that not every potential or current student of the instrument desires to become a concert pianist in a traditional classical style, Scott has developed an incredible ability to get anyone started in an extremely small amount of time using the techniques that professionals use to play non-classical music. A firm believer in the "a little more carrot and a lot less stick" approach to teaching piano, Scott continues to convert thousands of people worldwide into recreational music makers through his weekly series, his public television pledge specials, and live workshops. More information can be found at www.scottthepianoguy.com

Bradley Sowash and Scott Houston in the studio during the taping of "The Piano Guy."

How To Use This Book

Scott: Any advice for our readers before we get started?

Bradley: Don't read this book!

Scott: Then how will they learn anything?

Bradley: They won't learn much JUST reading. In order to get the maximum benefit, it's important that they read AND play through all the examples.

Scott: Why is that?

Bradley: Because knowing about music is not the same as playing it. Listeners aren't interested in your understanding of music, they're interested in how you sound. In order to sound good, you have to understand the nuts and bolts of music but it's APPLYING that knowledge to the keyboard that results in good music.

Scott: I see... It's like sports. Understanding the rules doesn't necessarily mean you can play very well. Does this mean the reader will have to absorb a heap of dry, boring music theory?

Bradley: Dry, boring theory? Nope. This book is about "practical" music. The opening chapters introduce basic information about chord construction, which is important, since the piano is a "chording" instrument. After that, we get right to the good stuff. You'll get the theory, but in a real world "show me how to use it" kind of way.

Scott: Let's get started.

Bradley: Here we go!

Chapter 1 – How to Construct Chords

    Scott: *To get started, we need to realize and accept a well known truism: the vast majority of professional, working, non-classical pianists use lead sheets, which contain melodies and chord symbols, to learn and create personalized versions of well-known songs.*

               Therefore, knowing how to interpret the chord symbols found in lead sheets is an essential ingredient to being able to play like a pro.

In this chapter, we'll:
    1. learn how to build chords
    2. find which chords are the most useful chords, and
    3. see how to play chords in different positions

    Scott: *Understanding chords is such an important aspect of piano playing. Can you show us how to construct chords?*

    Bradley: *The two most common ways to build chords are "stacking thirds" which is quick and easy and "counting half steps" which is more precise.*

Stacking Thirds to Create Chords

Let take a look at how chords derive from a scale.

Here are the eight notes that make up the C scale.
Playing these notes means we are in the key of "C."

We can build a chord on any of these notes by stacking additional notes above it. The notes we are going to add are found by "skipping" up the scale.

For example, to create a C chord:

1. Start with the note C and skip every other note moving up the scale until you have 3 notes with which to work.

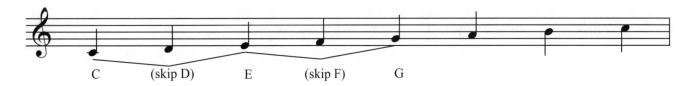

Specifically, keep the note C, (skip the note D), add the note E, (skip the note F), add the note G.

You end up with the notes C, E, and G.

2. Now, stack these notes one on top the other and you end up with a C chord. Here's how it looks in music notation:

And here's how it looks on the keyboard:

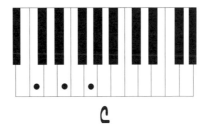

Musicians call this process *stacking thirds* because it involves adding every third note. It's like a picket fence where there's a slat (the note), then a space (the gap between notes), and then another slat and so on.

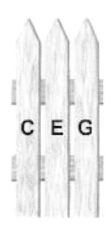

Notice that the notes in the chord are labeled root, 3rd and 5th. The root anchors the chord and gives it its name. The 3rd is 3 notes up from the root (C~D~E) and the 5th is 5 notes up from the root (C~D~E~F~G).

Scott: *And you can build a chord like this on any note of the scale?*

Bradley: *Sure - just pick a note and stack thirds.*

Suppose you wanted to build a chord with the note D as the root. Start with D and stack every other note above it moving up the scale.

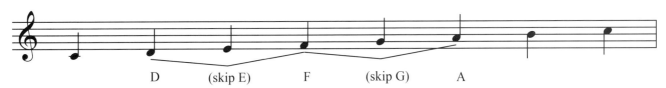

The result is a D minor chord.

7

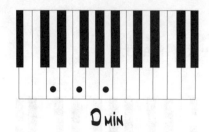

Continuing in this manner, we can build a chord on each note of the C major scale:

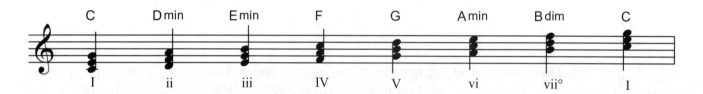

Scott: *What's with the Roman numerals?*

Bradley: *It's traditional to number chords using Roman numerals. Upper case numerals indicate major chords and lower case numerals indicate minor. The little degree sign indicates diminished chords.*

Scott: *Hold on a minute. Some of those chords are minor and I see a diminished chord. How do we know whether a chord is major, minor or diminished?*

Bradley: *By listening!*

A chord's quality (whether it is major, minor, or diminished) is sometimes referred to as its "flavor." Suppose you were blindfolded and someone handed you an ice cream cone. How would you figure out the flavor of the ice cream? You'd taste it! It's the same with chords. Play it and listen. If it is bright and cheery, you have a major chord. If it seems darker or sadder, you have a minor chord. Diminished chords, which are less common, sound downright eerie.

Play these three chord flavors and ask your ear to decide which is which.

The difference is even more pronounced if you compare chord qualities or flavors on the same root note. Play and compare these three chords which are all built on the root C:

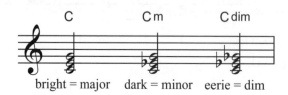

Here's a C in a chord diagram:

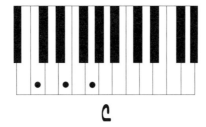

Here's a C min (note that the middle note is lower than the C chord above):

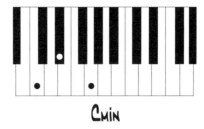

Here's a C dim (note that the top note is lower than the C min above):

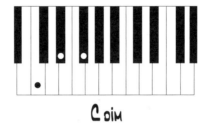

Keep these things in mind when using the stacked thirds method to build chords:

1. It's important to stay in the key when picking out chord tones. For example, in C major use only white keys. By doing this you'll play the right chord quality nine times out of ten because most of the chords in most songs use only notes associated with one key.

2. Use your ear. If you play the wrong chord, it will sound odd. Then you can make adjustments to make it sound right.

3. When a song calls for a chord that is not in the key (such as a chord in C major that requires a black key), it's usually the middle note (the 3rd) that needs adjusting up or down. Raise the 3rd to make a minor chord major. Lower the 3rd to make a major chord minor. Lower the 5th to make a minor chord diminished.

To sum up, build your chord initially by stacking thirds on the root (the name of the chord) while staying in the key. If it sounds wrong, alter the 3rd (or occasionally the 5th).

Scott: It makes sense. Now, what's this business I've heard about counting half steps to figure out chords?

Bradley: Suppose you are asked to play a chord and you don't know what key you are playing (like C major). Counting half steps is a fussier way to build a chord but it works.

Counting 1/2 Steps to Create Chords

Half steps are adjacent notes on the keyboard. For example, F to F# and Bb to B are both half step moves.

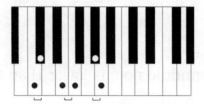

C-C#, E-F, and G#-A are all half step intervals because they are adjacent notes

A major chord has 4 half steps from the bottom note to the middle note and 3 half steps from the middle note to the top note.

Major Chord = Root, then up 4 half steps, then up 3 half steps

For example, suppose we wanted to create a F major chord...

Working from the bottom using the formula above, start on the Root F, then count up 4 half steps to get to A. (Since we are measuring the distance between notes, don't count the first note F.)

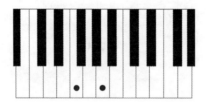

From F to A is 4 half step intervals, the "bottom" of a major chord

Now count up 3 half steps from the A to get to C:

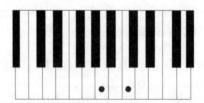

From A to C is 3 half step intervals, the "top" of a major chord

Put the two halves together to form an F major chord:

Put the "bottom" together with the "top" and you get a complete F major chord: F,A,C

The formula for a minor chord is simply reversed. Instead of starting on the root, then going up 4, then 3 half steps, we will start on the root, go up 3, then 4 half steps. (Clear as mud, eh? Actually, stick with me... it's not really that difficult to understand, just tough to describe on paper.)

A minor chord has 3 half steps from the bottom note to the middle note and 4 half steps from the middle note to the top note.

Minor Chord = Root, then up 3 half steps, then up 4 half steps

So, to create an F minor chord, start on the Root F, then count up 3 half steps to get to A-flat.

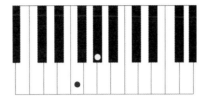

From F to A-flat is 3 half step intervals, the "bottom" of a minor chord

Now, count up 4 half steps from the Ab to get to C:

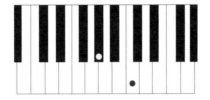

From A-flat to C is 4 half step intervals, the "top" of a minor chord

Put the two halves together and voila!: F minor:

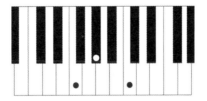

Put the "bottom" together with the "top" and you get a complete F minor chord: F, A-flat, C

Notice that the only difference between a major chord and minor chord is the middle note!

Scott: *So you can build chords by stacking thirds or counting half steps. Which is your favorite method?*

Bradley: *Whatever works for the student is best. Building chords is only a stepping stone. The ultimate goal is to memorize commonly used chords so we don't have to construct them time after time.*

Chapter 2 – Principal Chords, and Inversions

Scott: Alright, now that you know how to construct chords, you're probably thinking to yourself, "There are a lot of chords out there. How many do I really need to know to get started playing simple, well-known songs?" Here's the good news... With just three chords, you can play a whole truckload of music!

Principal Chords

Since any collection of simultaneous notes can theoretically be termed a chord, nearly an infinite number of chords are possible. We've touched on major, minor and diminished chords but we haven't even talked about augmented chords, 13th chords, flat 5 chords and a host of other scary sounding chord names. You, the student, may wonder, "so many chords, so little time?" Don't sweat it. It's helpful to realize that with just three important basic chords you have all you need to play "three chord" rock songs, folk music, holiday tunes, sacred tunes and songs that everybody knows like "On Top of Old Smoky."

Let's take another look at the chords that can be built on the C major scale:

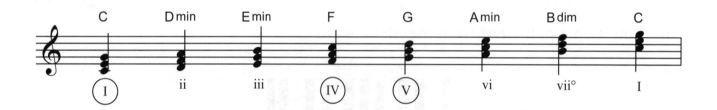

The chords we are most interested in are circled - those that are built on the 1st, 4th and 5th notes of the scale.

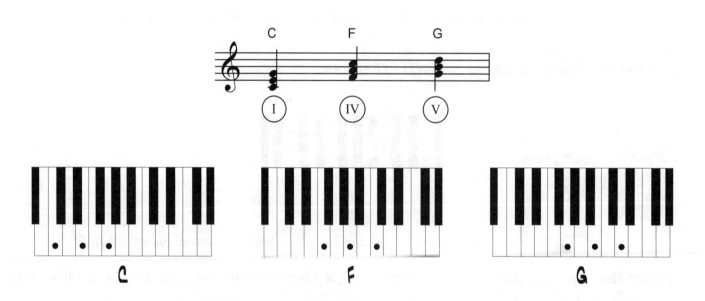

These chords are so versatile and useful that musicians call them *principal chords*. There are many, many wonderful melodies for which these three chords are all you need to create a satisfying accompaniment. And even in harmonically complex jazz songs, you are still likely to find these three chords mixed in with the rich, sophisticated chords that help define that musical style.

Scott: *These chords do have a familiar sound. Are we ready to use them in a song?*

Bradley: *We could use them as is but with one little change, we can make a significant enhancement.*

Seventh Chords

So far we've stacked thirds to create three note chords called triads. However, many lead sheets contain seventh chords. This is most often the case for the chord that is built on the 5th note of the scale. We call this the V chord (that's not V as in "vee" but rather V as in Roman Numeral 5). In the key of C major, it's a G chord. It's easy to convert this chord into a seventh chord - just stack another third on top.

The result looks like this:

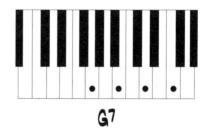

Notice that the chord symbol has changed to reflect this change. Adding a "7" to the chord symbol "G" to make "G7" indicates that there are seven notes from the bottom note to the top note (G-A-B-C-D-E-F). You could also call this the V7 chord (again, spoken as "five-seven," not "vee-seven").

Scott: *Why is the V chord the most likely to have another third stacked on top?*

Bradley: *The short answer is that it just sounds better. It has to do with the "tension and release" that help chords flow one to another. We'll learn more about that later...*

On the next page are the principal chords with the G chord changed to a G7 chord. Chords are most often played by the left hand in the lower portion of the piano (which is primarily notated in the bass clef in traditional notation.) For that reason, we will show you the chords notated in both the treble and bass clef.

13

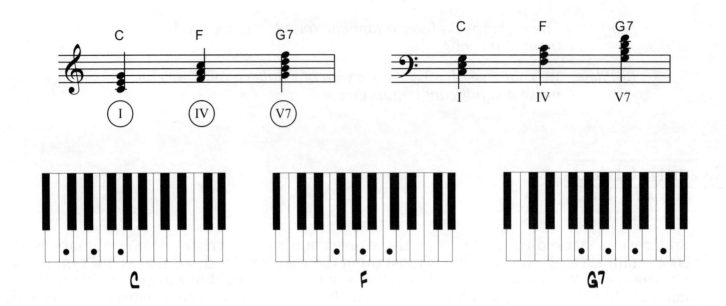

Putting Principal Chords to Work

You can play a lot of songs using just these three principal chords. Let's see how this would work on the old favorite, *On Top of Old Smoky*. Here's how this song looks in lead sheet form:

The first step to interpreting a lead sheet is to create a basic "skeletal" version. Using the principal chords, we could come up with something like you'll see on the following page:

On Top of Old Smoky

Traditional

"Skeleton" version with chords in root position

Scott: Sounds good but I notice the left hand jumps around a lot. How can we make it easier to play?

Bradley: By using inversions.

Inversions

You don't always have to play a chord with the root on the bottom. Chords can be played in various positions known as inversions. To create an inversion, move the bottom note of a chord to the top (one octave up).

For example, here are three positions of a C chord:

All of these C chords use the same notes (C, E, G) but each inversion has them in a different order. By the way, technically the first position is not really an inversion. It's just called root position.

Scott: How do we know which inversion to use when playing a chord?

Bradley: There are no rules about this. Unless the music specifies an inversion, you can play whatever position is easier to get to from the previous chord or whichever sounds best to you.

15

Slash Chords

Most of the time, a lead sheet with chord symbols will leave it up to the player to decide which inversion to use when playing a chord. However, sometimes a specific position is suggested through the use of slash chords.

The chord symbol "C/E" is an example of a slash chord. "C" indicates the name of the chord and "E" after the slash indicates that "E" is supposed to be on the bottom. Here are the C chord inversions expressed in slash chord symbols.

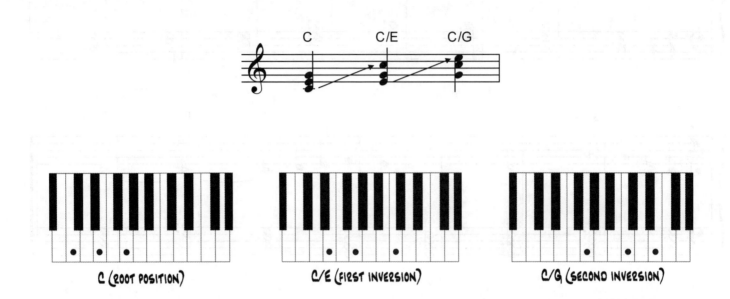

Pianists often use inversions to make it easier to move from one chord to another. Compare these two versions of the principal chords in the key of C. First, here they are in root position again just as we learned them:

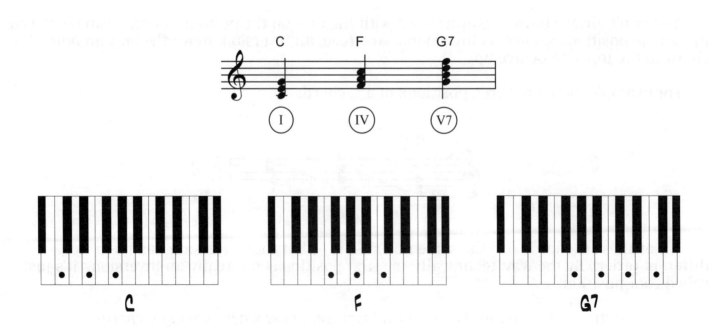

16

And here are the same chords in the most common inversions. The C chord is still in root position but notice the next two chords reorder the same notes as the previous example.

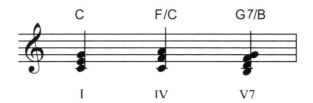

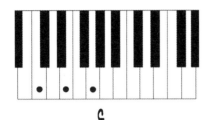 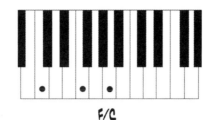 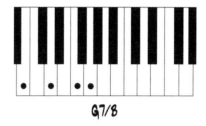

Here's a tip on playing 4 note chords: Since the four notes of the last chord (G7/B) are a handful compared to the three notes in the C and F chords, it's common to omit the second note up from the bottom (D) like this:

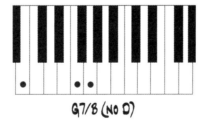

As it turns out, the D note we left out is the 5th of a G7 chord (G-A-B-C-D). It's kind of an "inside secret" that leaving out the 5th makes a chord more comfortable to play without changing the sound very much.

Here are the same chords simply notated down one octave in bass clef:

17

Let's put this concept of inversions to work in a song. Here's *Smoky* again with the principal chords in their most common inversions:

On Top of Old Smoky

(Principal chords using inversions)

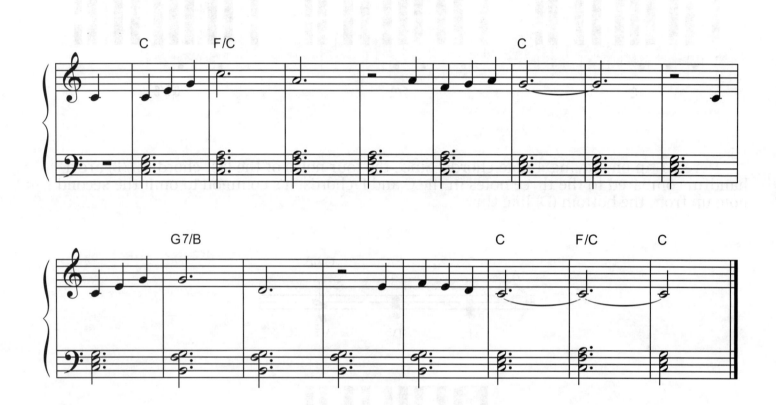

Notice how much easier this second version is to play. That's the power of inversions!

Chapter 3 - Left Hand Patterns and Basslines

>*Scott: This is a chapter for your left hand. In it, we'll learn some classic left hand patterns including one that was favored by Mozart. We'll also take a look at basslines. Both will give your piano playing a fuller, richer sound.*

We'll use *On Top of Old Smoky* as a basis for exploring ways to fill out the left hand so it's important that you can play it quite well before continuing. It is on the previous page, so take a look again for review.

>*Scott: Okay, we can play* Smoky *using principal chords in the left hand and a melody in the right hand. How do we go from here to get to the rich sound we hear when professional pianists play?*
>
>*Bradley: By adding motion to make a full accompaniment!*

Broken Chords

This version of *Smoky* is a "skeletal" interpretation of the lead sheet. It's important to go through this step of working out the basics when putting together a new song. The next step for a professional pianist would be to create a moving accompaniment to give it a feeling of forward motion.

The easiest way to do this is to use broken chords. Up until now, we've played the notes in chords simultaneously. To play a broken chord, simply play the notes in a chord one after another. It's like the chord breaks up into its three component notes.

Here how this would work on a C chord:

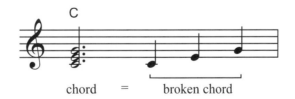

It's a good idea to position your fingers as if you are going to play the whole chord at once. That way, you can just drop your fingers in one by one.

Here are some more examples of broken chords on the F and G7 in their most common principal chord inversions:

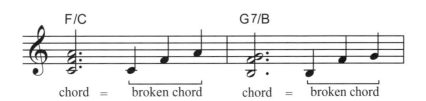

We can greatly enhance *On Top of Old Smoky* by simply changing the formerly "simultaneous note" chords to broken chords. Notice that none of the positions have moved. Everything is the same except that the notes of the chords sound one after another in a rolling motion:

On Top of Old Smoky

Traditional

Moving chords

Scott: *That's a neat trick! The broken chords really create a sense of forward motion. However,* On Top of Old Smoky *is in 3/4 time with 3 beats to the measure. Most tunes are in 4/4 time. How do you play broken chords in a tune with 4 beats to the measure?*

Bradley: *We can do it by borrowing a trick that a guy named Domenico Alberti worked out nearly 300 years ago.*

Broken Chords in Common Time

Playing broken major chords in 3/4 time does work out quite nicely because there are three notes in each chord and three beats in which to play them. To play broken chords in 4/4 time, we have to repeat a note.

A very effective pattern is as follows:
  1. bottom note
  2. top note
  3. middle note
  4. top note

20

Here's how it would work on a C chord:

We can also play the pattern twice as fast. By using 8th notes instead of quarters, we can squeeze two patterns into four beats:

Domenico Alberti ca. (1710 - 1740) used this pattern so extensively that they named it after him. You can also hear Alberti Bass frequently in the works of Franz Joseph Haydn, Wolfgang Amadeus Mozart, and early Ludwig van Beethoven.

Here is the Alberti Bass on the F and G7 principal chord inversions:

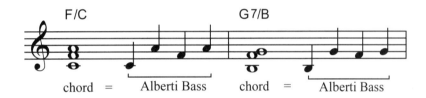

Let's see how this would work on a tune. Mozart wrote a set of variations to *Twinkle, Twinkle Little Star* for which he used Alberti Bass so it's appropriate that we explore it here.

Here's how it would look in lead sheet form:

21

The first step is always to work out a skeletal rendition. Try to do so now using principal chord inversions just by looking at the previous lead sheet. After you've done so, you can check yourself with the written version below:

Twinkle, Twinkle Little Star

Traditional

Skeleton version with principal chord inversions

A quick reminder...

It's okay to use inversions (such as on the F and G7 chords) even though the lead sheet does not indicate slash chord symbols (F/C or G7/B). You are always free to choose your own inversions when playing from a lead sheet. The only time you have to play a particular inversion is when it is specifically indicated by slash chord symbols.

Now, let's apply the Alberti Bass pattern to *Twinkle*. Using the same chord inversions as the skeletal version above, it should look and sound like this:

Twinkle, Twinkle Little Star

Traditional

Skeleton version with principal chord inversions

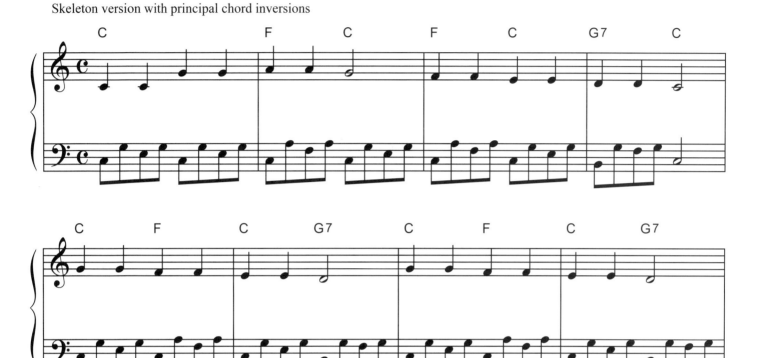

Scott: *Doesn't it sound great? It just proves that you don't have to be a genius to sound like one. All we need now is a powdered wig. What are some other ways to fill out the left hand?*

Bradley: *There must be a million ways to play chords. You can see how this is possible when you realize that chords can be spread out all over the piano.*

Chord Tones Are Everywhere

The notes in a chord are called chord tones. The chord tones in a C chord are the notes, C, E, and G.

We already know that this is a C chord:

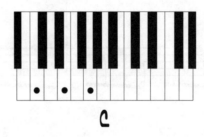

But this is also a C chord:

And so is this:

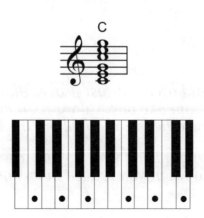

24

And even this is a C chord - impossible for one person to play, but you get the idea:

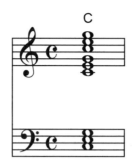

All of these are examples of C chords because they have the C chord tones (the notes C, E, and G). It doesn't matter how the notes are spread out or if they are doubled. If you play the notes C, E, and G in any configuration, you have a C chord.

Scott: *Very interesting but how is this useful?*

Bradley: *Left hand patterns and basslines rely on chord tones so it's useful to know that these notes are available all over keyboard.*

Basslines

Basslines add richness to a song due to their low resonance. In order to incorporate basslines into our playing, we need to understand their characteristics:

1. Basslines are the lowest notes in an arrangement. The lowest note in the left hand is heard as a bassline even when it's the bottom note of a chord.

2. Basslines typically stick to chord tones. Imagine a guitar and bass duet. If the guitarist played a C chord and the bassist played the note Db, it would sound awful. To sound good, the bassist might choose to play the root of the C chord (the note C). (He/She could also choose other chord tones such as the notes E or G. However, basslines most often stick to the roots of chords particularly on the heavy beats.)

3. Basslines typically move slower than the melody. They plod along holding up the bottom end of the music.

4. Basslines change on the heavy beats. In Western music, more weight is given to the downbeat, which is the first beat in a measure. Sing the song, *Yankee Doodle*, out loud and you'll notice that you tend to unconsciously emphasize the downbeats:

YAN-kee Doodle **WENT** to town **RID**-ing on a **PO**-ny...

Without this emphasis on the downbeat of each measure, it would sound like a run on sentence:

Yankeedoodlewentottownridingonapony...

Since chords often change on downbeats and basslines emphasize chord tones, basslines usually change on downbeats as well. To be specific, basslines can change notes more often, but they surely change notes on the heavy beats.

Creating a Bassline by Changing Inversions

Let's see how we can combine our knowledge of basslines and chord tones to add a bassline to *On Top of Old Smoky*. Here are the first few measures of the skeletal version:

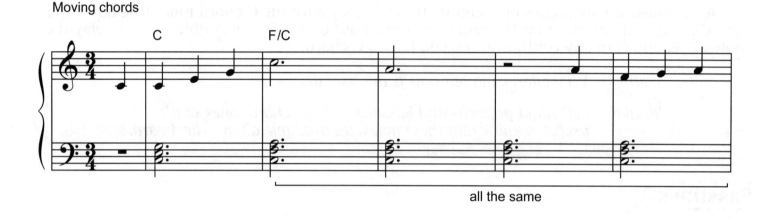

Notices that the F chords in the last four measures of the left hand are all alike - the same chord in the same inversion. We can add interest by changing inversions on the F chord like this:

Something very interesting happens when we do this. The ear tends to hear the bottom note of these changing chord tones on downbeats as if it were a bassline that sounds like this:

To the listener, it sounds like three things are happening - a melody, accompanying chords, and a bassline. This is a very important aspect of solo piano playing and we'll learn more about it in a later chapter.

For now, use this trick on the whole song, and you'll come up with something like this:

On Top of Old Smoky

Traditional

Moving chords in root position with bass notes between

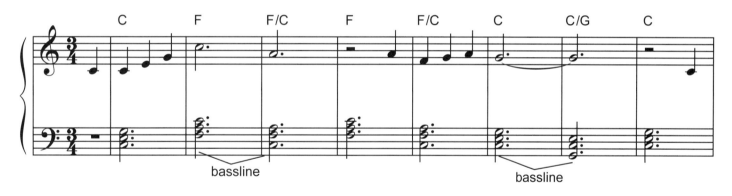

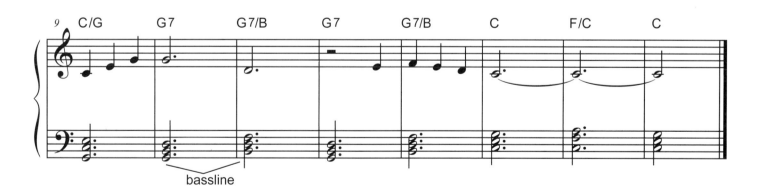

27

Now, we add motion back in and we really have something:

Scott: It sounds good but it's a little tough to play with the left hand moving around so much.

Bradley: So we'll simplify it! There's always an easier way.

Keep the top two notes of the inversions the same while still varying the bassline. It sounds just as good but it's less difficult:

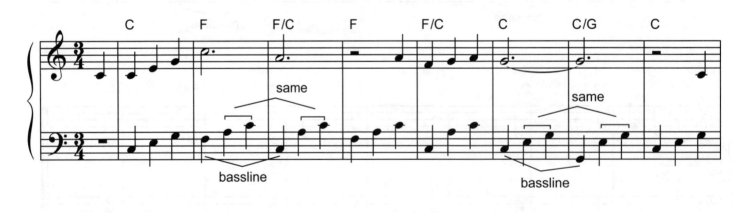

Passing Note Bass

A neat way to turn bass notes into a bassline is to connect the chords by using passing notes. These are the notes that "point" to the root of the upcoming chord by moving in its direction.

For example, suppose we had a C chord moving to an F chord. We could create a bassline by filling in the passing notes between:

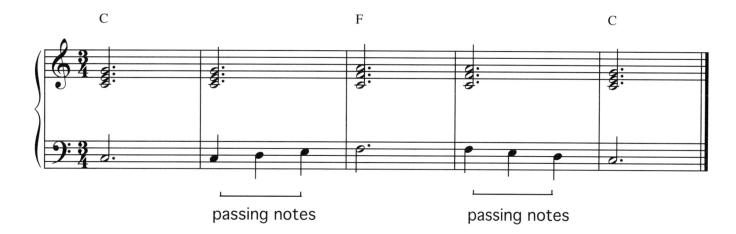

The rules for creating passing note basslines are simple. Play the root of the chord you are leaving (C) on the downbeat and then fill in the notes that point to the new chord (F).

Let's see how this would work in "*Smoky.*"

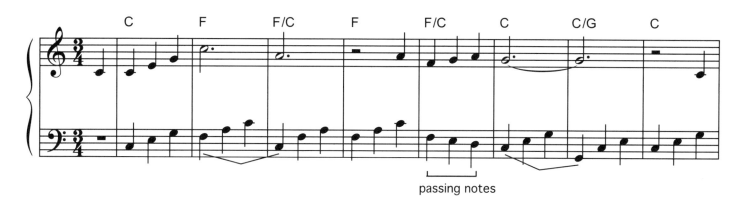

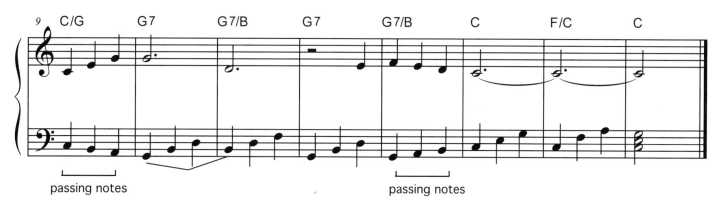

See how the passing note bass further enhances this old chestnut? The left hand can do so much more than just pound out chords.

29

Chapter 4 – Embellishing the Melody

Scott: *All right gang, we need to keep going and dig a little deeper! You are about to learn another bassline technique as well as how to personalize a melody.*

Scott: *Let's talk about the right hand. What else does it do besides play the melody?*

Bradley: *The right hand personalizes a song through embellishment.*

    First, let me say that melody matters a lot! A lot of musicians forget that. For most listeners, the melody is their way into a song. Recognizing the melody helps the listener appreciate your rendition of a particular song. So it's important to play the melody up front in the beginning of a song.

    Let's use a different song to explore melodic possibilities. Here's an old favorite in lead sheet form:

30

This one is in the key of G major, which means all the F notes are automatically played as F#s. Here are the chords you will need in root position:

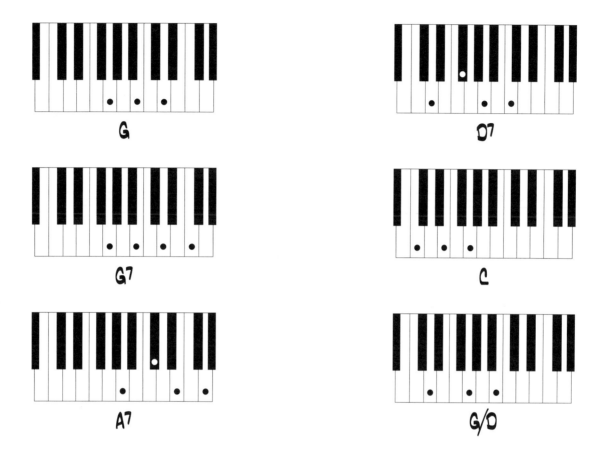

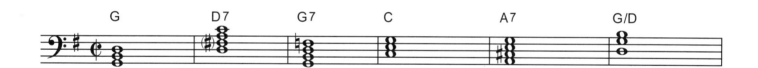

You know what to do next - work out the skeletal version with chords in the left hand. Do it by yourself first and then check yours against the written version on the next page.

She'll Be Comin' 'Round the Mountain

Folk Song

Was your version similar? Don't worry if it varied somewhat. Perhaps you used different chord inversions? No matter. As long as you are able to pick out the left hand chords and play them with the right hand melody, you are in good shape.

Scott: *I bet some of our readers are already thinking about ways to add motion using the left hand patterns such as Alberti Bass that we discussed in the previous chapter.*

Bradley: *...And those approaches would work quite well on this tune. However, this is a good opportunity to introduce another type of bassline for the left hand. It's easy to play, so it frees up more brain power to concentrate on the right hand.*

EZ Bassline

Basslines in old time songs like this one often emphasize the root and 5th chord tones. *Comin' 'Round the Mountain* begins on a G chord. The root of a G chord is the note G and the 5th of a G chord is the note D.

Play the root followed by the 5th in the left hand.

I call this type of root and 5th pattern EZ Bass. It's useful for many older styles of music such as marches, fiddle tunes, bluegrass, ethnic styles and more.

Like most basslines, it's important to play the root (G) on the downbeat. From there, you can move down or up to the 5th (D).

In fact, you can mix them up:

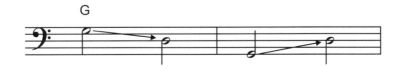

33

Try replacing the left hand chords in *Comin' 'Round the Mountain* with an EZ bassline. Here's one possibility:

She'll Be Comin' 'Round the Mountain

Folk Song

Learn to play this or something close to it very well - maybe even memorize it before going on.

Scott: Okay, tell us about embellishment? It sounds like a culinary term.

Bradley: It's just a fancy way of describing the process of customizing a melody to "make it your own."

If you sang *Comin' 'Round the Mountain* as a kid, you probably didn't sing it quite so squarely as it's written here with steady quarter notes. Try humming a few measures right now without giving much thought to the written music. The chances are that your memory of this song uses somewhat different rhythms than the written version. Now, see if you can play it on the piano just as you hummed it. You can use just your right hand or combine it with the left hand EZ Bass if that's not a challenge.

Scott: Whoa Nelly! Did you say to play the music differently from the way it is written? I can just imagine traditional piano teachers rolling over in their graves.

Bradley: Don't worry. They won't be stopping by to rap your knuckles with a ruler. Customizing the melody is totally appropriate for this style of music. You might even say it's wrong to play it exactly as written.

Scott: Let me get this straight... You're saying that it is not only OK, but that you SHOULD play a tune differently than it is written?

Bradley: If you ever want to sound authentic and professional – yes.

Here's the version I remember from camp:

Notice how the rhythm for the lyrics "comin' around" differ from the lead sheet version.

Scott: This is the version I remember as well. Why don't lead sheets show these familiar rhythms in the first place?

Bradley: Lead sheets are only intended as a **reference** so they are written in a simple format to make them easy to read. Also, not everyone will agree on the "correct" version so it's up to the musician to customize the music.

Children who are just learning to play an instrument often make these rhythmic adjustments naturally. They play what suits their ear. When the written music differs from the song as they know it or would like to hear it, they prefer to play what they hear in their head.

Of course, teachers often correct this since it leads to improper reading in the classical style but the unintended consequence is that students are discouraged from learning to interpret a melody in their own way. Musical styles such as jazz and folk music don't work that way. New interpretations are encouraged!

Scott: Okay, but most adults and some kids need more to think about than just "play what suits your ear." I get feedback all the time from people saying, "I just don't have it in me!" Can you give us some specific approaches to embellishing a melody?

Bradley: You are right that the goal is to play what you hear. But we can break it down in order to see the possibilities and suggest some concrete ways to get started down the path towards playing by ear.

1. Rhythmic Embellishment

Rhythms are an obvious place to begin. We've already adjusted them according to our memory of this song. Taking this idea further, we can deliberately change the rhythms by lengthening, shortening, omitting or repeating certain notes:

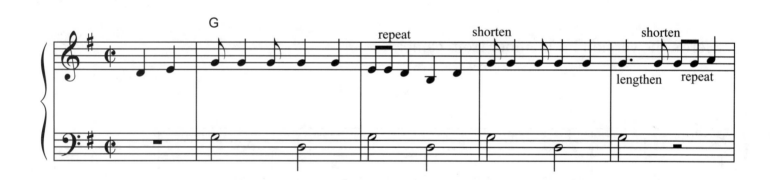

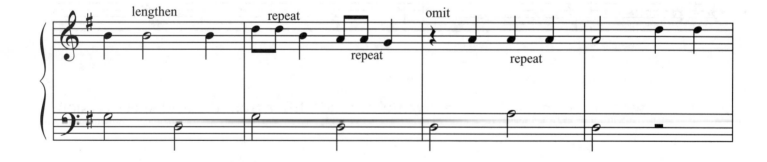

Now, I'd like you to play with the notes in this song to create your own rhythmic embellishments. Don't change the pitches for now. Just see what you come up with by lengthening, shortening, omitting or repeating certain notes. Here's the EZ Bass version you learned or memorized earlier for reference but play the right hand rhythms differently than what is written.

36

She'll Be Comin' 'Round the Mountain

Folk Song

(Tic, toc, tic, toc... I'm waiting for you to actually play it. Don't cheat by just looking at it and going ahead.)

Did you do it? Congratulations. You've taken your first step towards developing your own style.

2. Melodic Embellishment

Another way to customize a song is to change or add new notes to the melody. I can hear you, the student, saying, "Yikes, what notes do I use?" And I understand why. This is kind of a wide-open territory that potentially gets into using a whole host of scales, modes, ornamentation and other musical devices that vary from style to style.

However, the simple key to melodic embellishment is to rely on the notes in the key signature. *Comin 'Round the Mountain* is in G major which means the melody and chords use the notes in the G major scale:

Change or add these notes to the melody and you'll be bound to sound good, at least most of the time. Here's an example:

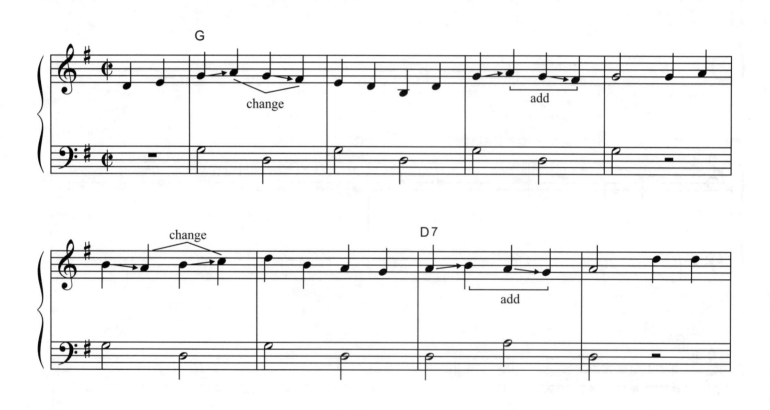

Scott: *Does this mean you have to use only the notes in the G major scale when you embellish a melody?*

Bradley: *Absolutely not! If you want to go further without opening the Pandora's box of every note on the piano, look to chord tones.*

3. Chord Tone Embellishment

If you really want to sound like you know what you are doing, make a point of bringing out chord tones (the notes in the chord) when embellishing a melody. They are intelligent note choices, since any note that is in a chord will sound good in the melody above it.

Since we've been relying on the EZ Bass so far, the actual chords to *Comin' 'Round the Mountain* may have grown fuzzy in your mind. However, we have to know the chords in order to emphasize chord tones in our melodic embellishment. The example below helps because it shows the chords specified by the lead sheet in their root positions. The chords are the whole notes, which are followed by the melody. Your job is to create a melodic embellishment that emphasizes these chord tones. To do so, simply mix some of the notes from the chords into the written melody. Use this example to get yourself started and then try some variations of your own.

39

Scott: Nice, but it sounds fairly different from the recognizable melody. When should you use embellishments?

Bradley: It's a good idea for the listener's sake to play the melody somewhat "straight" the first time through a song and then add embellishments for interest on the repeat. It's part of how you transform a 16-measure song into a longer performance.

4. Putting Embellishments Together

Having learned about rhythmic, melodic and chord tone embellishments, we can mix them freely together to enhance the melody as in this example:

40

Scott: *So do professional pianists think to themselves, "I'll move the rhythm here, and then do a scale run followed by some chord tones..." putting together an embellished melody intellectually?*

Bradley: *They may practice this way but experience enables them to embellish almost unconsciously in performance.*

Like painters who try to "see" a finished picture in their mind's eye, improvising pianists are concerned with trying to play what they "hear" in their mind's ear. To be able to do this, the first step is to have plenty of musical ideas. This comes by listening attentively and then emulating a musical style that interests you.

The second step is to find the notes that match those you are hearing in your head. Knowing which notes are likely to "fit" (key signature and chord tones) in a given song makes it easier to find them.

Now that you have these techniques under your belt, go back and play through the EZ Bass version as it is written. Then repeat it a few times embellishing the right hand by loosening up the rhythms and adding or changing notes using the G major scale and chord tones. Don't worry if your playing doesn't exactly match what you are hearing. If you don't like what you hear, try something else! Playing piano in this non-classical style is not an exercise in perfection.

Experiment. Play around. Try things. This is why they call it "playing" piano instead of "working" piano. But to get better at playing, you need to play more. Really do it!

Understanding musical concepts is not the same as playing them. If you can add playing embellishments to your bag of tricks, you'll be having more fun at the piano and be that much closer to sounding like a professional musician.

CHAPTER 5 – ADDING FILLS AND IMPROVISING

Scott: What musicians haven't dreamed of flying on their own power playing whatever their hearts desire? This chapter will help you chart a course into the wild blue skies of creativity at the keyboard.

Scott: What is improvisation anyway?

Bradley: Improvisation is the art of making music spontaneously without the aid of written music.

Scott: A lot of people think you have to be a great talent to improvise.

Bradley: That's because they believe improvisation relies solely on "I was just born with it..." when actually, there are specific steps that enable one to get started making music through improvisation.

Consider that we all improvise everyday by having conversations. Imagine an acquaintance approaches and asks, "Hello, how are you?" Do you have to consult a written script to reply? Not at all. Rather, you draw on previously learned phrases and your familiarity with language to construct a response. Depending on our personal style, it may be "Just fine, thank you" or "I'm cool, dude" or "All my systems are fully functional."

The point is that music is like language in that it exists in both written and aural forms. You can read written music just like you can read a novel. And you can play music without written assistance just like you can speak without a script.

Scott: Then why is it that some quite accomplished musicians find improvisation frightening. Is it really that hard?

Bradley: Some serious musicians have had the creativity trained right out of them. By becoming experts at reproducing the written note and always worrying about not playing "wrong" notes, they've forgotten how to just play around with music.

Scott: So, improvisation is really not that hard for the emerging player?

Bradley: If you asked someone to blindly improvise with no direction, it would be a tall order. But if you break it down by showing them where to improvise and which notes will fit, it's wonderful fun!

To see how improvisation works, let's learn a new song. *When the Saints Go Marching In* is a classic melody which has been in continual favor since the earliest days of jazz right up until the present day. Here it is in lead sheet form:

When the Saints Go Marching In

Traditional

Here are all the chords to *When the Saints Go Marching In* with the inversions we suggest to make playing this song smoother and easier.

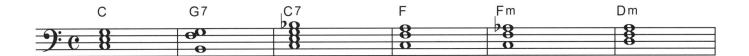

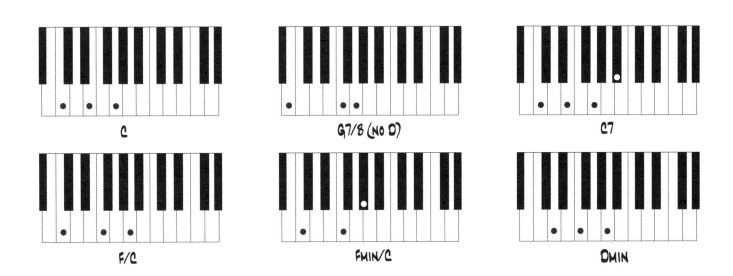

Putting these chords together with the melody, we can create a skeletal version that looks and sounds something like this:

When the Saints Go Marching In

Traditional

We'll use this version as a basis for exploring improvisation. Practice it until you can play it quite well before going on.

Scott: *Why have jazz musicians been attracted to this song for so long?*

Bradley: *Because it is a perfect vehicle for improvisation, which is the very heart of jazz.*

Fills

A good way to start improvising is to fill in the slow spots within a melody. Take another look at the first few measures of *Saints*. The spaces after the whole notes in the 2nd and 4th measures are dead spots where the music just sits as if waiting for the next phrase to begin.

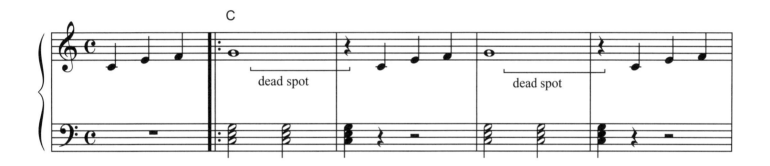

In the early days of Dixieland music, the trumpet would often play the melody while the clarinet filled in spots like this with improvisations.

Scott: *Now, here is the million-dollar question: Fill it in with what?*

Bradley: *When in doubt, pent out!*

Scott: *You jazz players are so weird...*

Bradley: *Read on my friend!*

The Pentatonic Scale

Musicians around the world favor this scale in their improvisations. It's similar to the major scale except that it has a couple of notes missing.

C Major Scale

C Major Scale with notes missing:

C Pentatonic Scale:

The C major scale without the 4th note (F) and 7th note (B) is the pentatonic scale: C, D, E, G and A. These five notes have the mysterious property of sounding good over a variety of chords in just about any musical style. Try noodling around with these five notes with just your right hand. An easy way to think of it is all the white keys except for the notes F and B. You don't have to play them in order. Start on any note and go up or down.

Continue with your own:

Regardless of how you order them, they sound fine. When improvising, these notes are like your five best friends. Even master improvisers who use a lot of different scales and patterns rely on the pentatonic scale as a good fallback scale that will work most of the time.

Try filling in the dead spots in *Saints*. Play the melody as written but add fills when the melody hits a dead spot. Here's an example to get you started. The notes in the fills are smaller to distinguish them from the main melody.

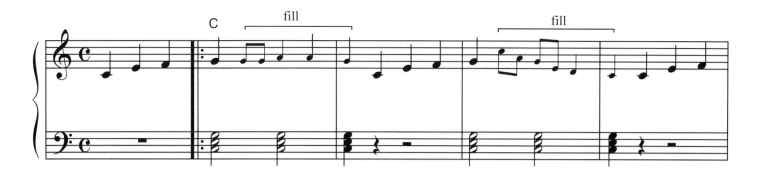

Now you try it. Use the notes in the C pentatonic scale (C, D, E, G, A). Remember that there's no right or wrong way to do this.

Filling with Chord Tones

Looking ahead to the next line in *Saints*, we come to another dead spot on the G7 chord.

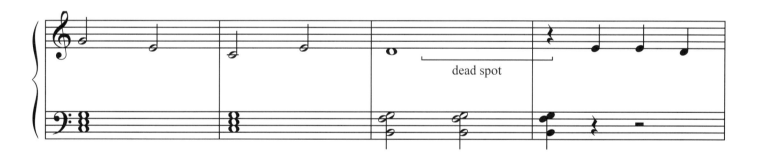

Playing a fill that uses notes from the pentatonic scale would work here (pentatonic works almost anywhere) but there's a better choice. The G7 chord contains the notes B and F, which are the very C major scale notes that are missing from the pentatonic scale.

Improvising is not unlike embellishing. It just takes it further. We learned in the last chapter that the notes within a chord also sound good in an embellishment above it.

Applying the same principle here, we can create a fill that emphasizes the chord tones (G, B, D, F) in a G7 chord for a better fit.

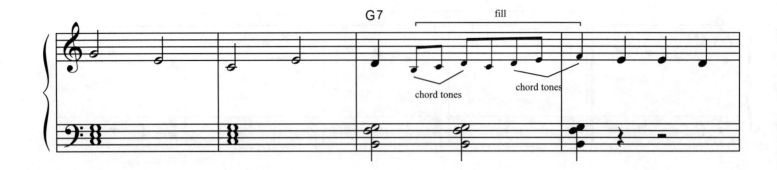

Now you try it. Play a fill that uses some or all of the chord tones (G, B, D, F) in a G7 chord.

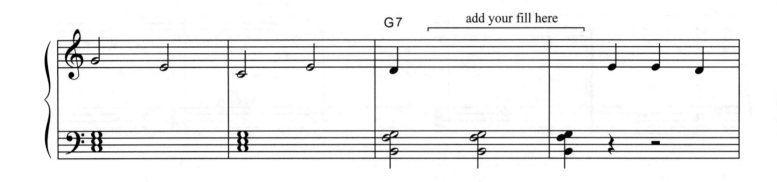

Scott: *So when do you use the pentatonic scale and when do you use chord tones?*

Bradley: *Use the pentatonic scale all the time. Use chord tones more selectively whenever you can.*

Let's be clear:

1. The Pentatonic scale can be used anytime for improvising.
   When in doubt, pent out!
2. Use chords instead of (or in addition to) the pentatonic scale whenever you spot a note in a chord that is not in the pentatonic scale.

Scott: *What do jazz musicians mean when they talk about soloing? Does this mean that they play by themselves like a solo pianist?*

Bradley: *That is confusing. Playing alone is indeed one meaning of the word, solo. However, a jazz solo refers to the time when a musician improvises without regard for the original composed melody. This can occur while playing alone or with an ensemble.*

The Jazz Solo

Louis Armstrong was one of the first great geniuses of jazz. When he was asked how he constructed a solo, he replied, "First I play the melody, then I 'routines' the melody, then I routines the routines." By "routines the melody," I think he was referring to embellishing the melody and adding fills. But when he said, "routines the routines," he was talking about the jazz solo in which musicians freely create their own melodic line while dispensing with the composed melody altogether. Here's a sample improvised solo:

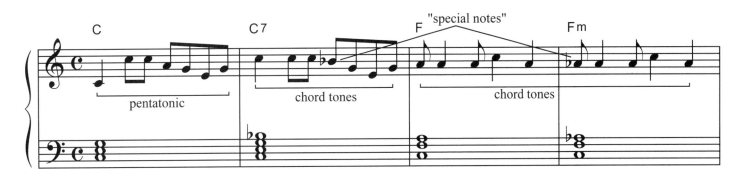

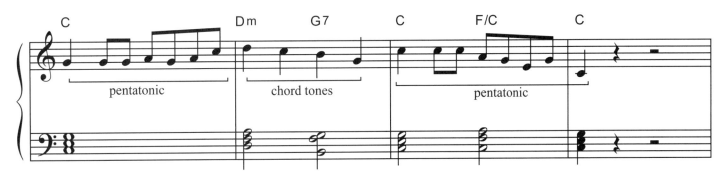

Now, you try it. Improvise a right hand part over these chords. Think pentatonic (C, D, E, G, A) and chord tones. Here's a tip: if a chord has accidentals (notes that are not in the key signature), it's a good idea to include those notes in your improvisation. In other words, if you know there's a sharp or flat in the chord, use it in your solo above it. For example, the C7 chord has the note Bb in it. The Fm chord has the note Ab in it. Think of these as "special notes" that you can choose to bring out.

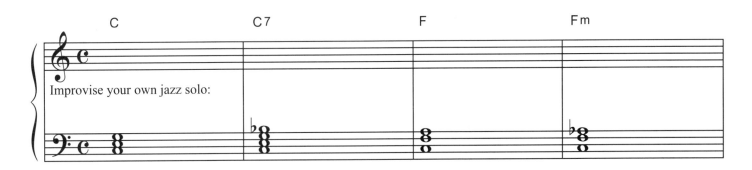

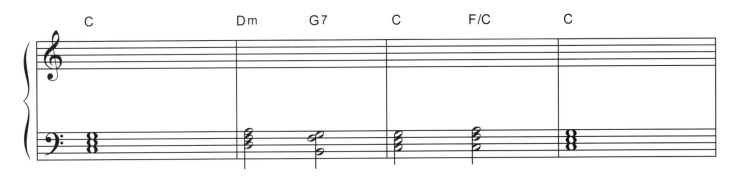

Scott: *Okay, we have the melody, embellishments, fills and jazz solos. How do we use all that to perform a song?*

Bradley: *Take Louie's advice!*

Putting it all together by following Louie's advice, we might come up with something like this:

1. "First, I play the melody..." - play a fairly straight version all the way through. Let the listener hear and recognize the melody.

2. "...then I routines the melody..." - embellish the melody and/or add fills to suit your taste.

3. "...then I routines the routines..." - improvise a jazz solo without regard to the composed melody.

4. Louis didn't say it, but it is customary to return to some or all of the melody after soloing, usually in a grander or somehow more enhanced fashion.

Now you try it. Here's *Saints* with all of the various parts to use as a reference. Fill in the right-hand blank areas with your own fills and improvisations but also feel free to vary your left hand rhythms. Try to play what you hear.

Here's a very freeing thought to remember long beyond this particular example in this particular book:

> If you play something you don't mean that still sounds good, your audience will never know the difference. Think of it this way: <u>there are no wrong notes</u> - just better or worse ones.
>
> That's the beauty of improvising! Knowing the key signature and chord tones only helps to insure a higher percentage of finding the best notes.

When the Saints Go Marching In

Traditional

How did it go? Were you able to play what you were hearing at least part of the time? When you played something other than what you were hearing, did it sound bad?

CHAPTER 6 – COMBINING MELODY, HARMONY AND BASS

Scott: *This is an important chapter. Here, you'll learn some tricks of the trade about how to get a solo piano to sound like a group of musicians. You'll also pick up some musical styles along the way. Dig in and have fun.*

Scott: *Why do pianists often play by themselves?*

Bradley: *Because they can...*

The Elements of Music

The piano has been considered a versatile solo instrument since its earliest days. That's because the piano is one of the only instruments capable of handling all the elements of music.

We don't often encounter a solo flutist playing in a fancy hotel lobby. The flute is a great melodic instrument. However, because it plays just one note at a time in a high range, it's incapable of producing chords or basslines. Likewise, zither players are not usually soloists due to the limitations of their chords-only instrument. Bassists, who cover the bottom end of the spectrum, rarely play chords or melodies. These instruments are usually heard in combination with others, each playing a unique role to fill out the elements of music. Listeners are accustomed to hearing music played by ensembles such as a small jazz combo, rock band or orchestra with several instruments handling various elements of the music.

Therefore, in order to sound convincing, the solo pianist has to suggest the following three elements of music:

1. Melody
2. Harmony (chords)
3. Bass

Here's a version of *Twinkle, Twinkle Little Star* with all three elements in place:

(D.C. al Fine means to repeat the first four measures at the end stopping at Fine.)

54

Scott: I see the problem - three tasks to perform with only two hands.

Bradley: Exactly. It's not really possible for one pianist to keep the melody, chords and basslines running all at the same time. However, throughout the history of music, pianists have become adept at convincing us that all three are present. Let's explore some of the ways they have done that.

Right Hand Combo

One way to get a melody, harmony and bass going all at the same time is to combine two of these elements in the same hand. Melodies are almost always played by the right hand so that's a given. The left hand necessarily covers basslines because it plays down on the low end of the piano where basslines live. That leaves harmony as the musical wild card that can be played by either hand. Let's see how it's possible to combine the melody and harmony in just the right hand.

55

Begin by playing just the melody to *Twinkle* with just your right hand pinky (5) finger.

The next step is to fill in the chords below the melody note. To do this, you must choose a chord inversion that has the melody note on top.

Here are the three positions for a C chord:

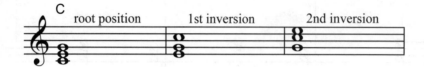

Here are the three positions for an F chord:

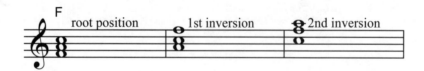

G7 has four notes, so there are four positions:

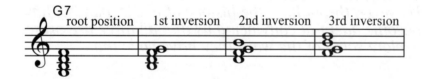

Twinkle begins with two C notes in the melody under a C chord symbol. A quick check of the C chord positions above reveals that the 1st inversion has C as the top note. By adjusting the octave down, we find that this chord fits under the first two notes of the melody.

The melody continues with two G notes still under a C chord symbol. Another check back reveals G as the top note of a C chord in root position. So we drop it in.

The second measure of *Twinkle* has two A notes in the melody under an F chord symbol. Find the position of an F chord with an A on top and you have it.

Continue throughout the melody and you'll come up with this right hand part:

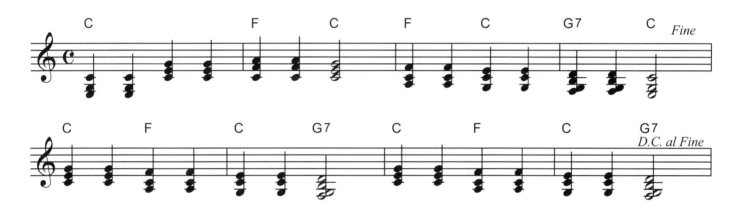

When you can play this, add this simple bass line:

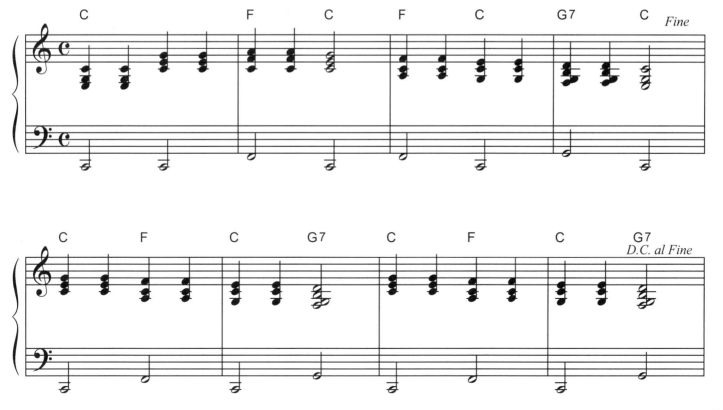

57

Voila! You've successfully combined all three elements of music - melody and chords in your right hand and a bassline in your left.

Scott: *That's a great technique. The music sounds full and complete.*
           Do you always have to play a chord on every melody note?

Bradley: *You can actually do whatever you want.*

How you decide to integrate harmony into the melody is a question of taste and practicality. Play through the next version of *She'll Be Comin' 'Round the Mountain* and observe the following:

1. Since this is an uptempo song, it's easier to place the right hand chords on every other beat unlike Twinkle where we put a chord on every melody note.

2. In the second measure, there's a non-chord tone, which is a melody note that is not in the chord. The G chord is made up of the notes G, B, D but the melody note is an E which is not in this chord. No problem, we just play some of the G chord as we can fit it in below it.

3. You don't always have to play complete chords. It's fine just to play one or two notes of a three-note chord such as the second measure of the second line.

She'll Be Comin' 'Round the Mountain

Folk Song

Scott: We've seen how the right hand can combine the melody and harmony. Is it possible to play a bassline and harmony in the left hand?

Bradley: Oh, there are lots of ways to accomplish that. Actually, we've already seen a few with the broken chords and Alberti Bass patterns. We'll explore some other left hand patterns once we've learned a bit about open and closed chords.

Open and Closed Broken Chords

A chord is closed when the chord tones are as close together as possible. Here is a C chord in closed position:

C (closed) = [musical notation: C chord]

The notes C, E, and G are stacked up one on another so they cannot be any closer.

Inversions don't effect whether a chord is open or closed. All of these chords are in closed position:

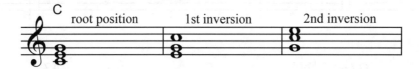

Open position means the chord tones are spread out as in this example:

C (open) = [musical notation and keyboard diagram]

Notice that the chord tones C, E, and G are arranged so that they skip every other possibility. C is the first and lowest note. Then, we skip over the next possible chord tone which is an E (shown with an X). We keep the next note G, skip the next chord tone C (shown with an X) and finish with the note E. The effect is plenty of space between the chord tones.

Left Hand Combos

Now, we'll move on to the good stuff. The rest of this chapter demonstrates left hand patterns that combine harmony and bass in the same hand. Let's pick a new song as a basis for putting closed and open chords to work in left hand combos. *Amazing Grace* is one of the best-loved songs of all time. Here it is in lead sheet form:

By now, you should know how to create a skeletal version on your own so we'll just get you started with the left hand chords you will need.

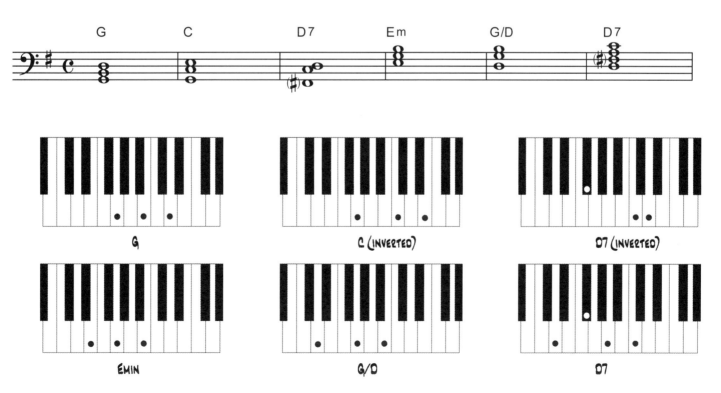

61

Use these chords to create a skeletal version. We are not providing a written version to check it against. You are on your own. Don't cheat. Really do it! When you've got it under your fingers, move on to these variations.

Broken Chords

Just as we did with *On Top of Old Smoky*, you can add motion to *Amazing Grace* by using broken chords in closed position like this:

Amazing Grace

Traditional

The first note in the left hand of each measure implies a bassline by sounding the root and the rest of the measure outlines the chord. The result sounds good but we can enhance it further in two ways:

1. Mixed Broken Chords (open and closed)

First play an open chord (G, D, B) and then follow it with a closed chord (G, B, D). This gives the left hand a nice flowing sound that covers a lot of range on the piano.

2. Passing Note Bass

Remember that you can play passing note basslines between chord changes. Start with the root of the chord you are leaving (G) on the downbeat and then fill in the notes that point to the new chord (C).

The version on the next page alternates between these mixed open and closed broken chords and passing note basslines:

Amazing Grace

Traditional

Scott: *That's a great pattern for playing in 3/4 time that's worth memorizing for future use. Is there a similar pattern in 4/4 time?*

Bradley: *Sure. We do it by adding a few notes to fill out the time.*

Open and Closed Broken Chords in 4/4 Time

Here's an open and closed pattern for a C chord that works with 4 beats to the measure which is also called common time.

We can apply this pattern to our old friend, *Twinkle*, by slowing down the melody in order to fit it all in.

Twinkle, Twinkle Little Star

Traditional

Etc.

Notice how the flowing character of this pattern changes the feel of the song to a beautiful ballad.

65

Stride

Another popular way to get bass and harmony into the left hand is to simply alternate them. The usual pattern is to play a low octave bass note on the root (C), then the chord, then the 5th (G), and then the chord.

The root and 5th provide a bassline and the chords in between take care of the harmony. If there are two chords in one measure, you only play the roots (leave out the 5th).

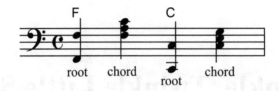

Jazz musicians call this left hand style "stride piano" but it was around long before jazz was invented. You'll find it in the works of Haydn, Beethoven, and Chopin to name a few.

Scott: *Now that's a familiar sound but it's tough to play with all that left hand "target practice." Is there an easier way?*

Bradley: *There's always an easier way...*

Faux Stride

It takes a lot of practice to get your left hand to hit all those low octaves and then bounce up to the chords. So let's eliminate the octave on beats 1 and 3 and play just the top half of the chords on beats 3 and 4.

To the casual listener, this simpler approach sounds much the same and it's much easier to play. Here's an example of how it would work in a song

Twinkle, Twinkle Little Star

Traditional

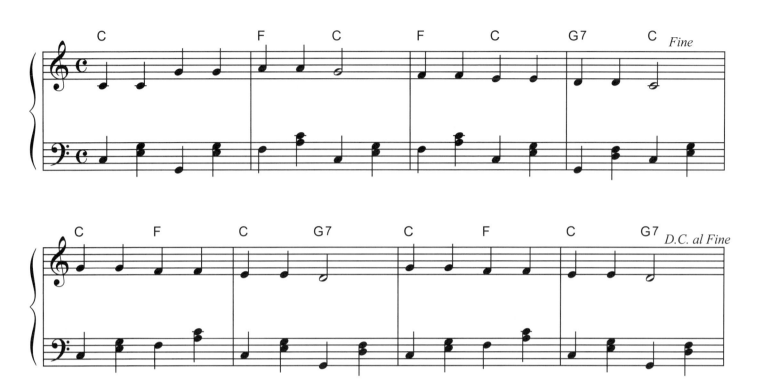

Scott: Okay, now I'll reverse my earlier question: That's a great pattern for playing in 4/4 time. How do you play stride piano in 3/4 time?

Bradley: Now you're talking about a waltz.

Waltz

The waltz is a song in 3/4 that evolved with a popular dance step of the 18th century. The dancer's weight is down on beat 1 and up on the tiptoes for beats 2 and 3. This "down, up, up" feel is built right into the music in a kind of modified stride (not that they called it that). It sounds like "oom-pah-pah."

The waltz pattern is a low octave bass note on the root (C), followed by two chords:

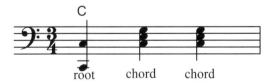

Where you have two measures with no chord changes, you alternate the root with the 5th:

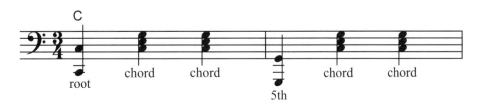

67

Faux Waltz

To simplify the pattern, eliminate the octave on beat 1 and play just the top half of the chords on beats 2 and 3.

Here it is in context:

Amazing Grace

Traditional

68

Chapter 7 – How Chords Function

Scott: Have you ever wondered why one chord sounds good but not another? This short chapter gets us into some very practical music theory that all musicians should understand, particularly pianists.

Chord Function

Chords are more than just pretty sounds. They actually *do* things like creating tension to move the music forward or releasing to bring the music to rest. We'll use a baseball diamond metaphor to explain how this works. Keep in mind that chord function is difficult to capture on paper so it's particularly important that you play and listen to the examples in this chapter.

Let's recall from Chapter 1, that chords are derived from scales.

C Major Scale:

Chords built on the C scale:

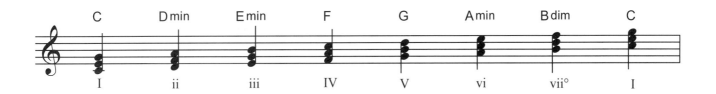

Remember that the three most used chords are called the principal chords.

C Major Principal Chords in Root Position:

69

Home Base - The I Chord

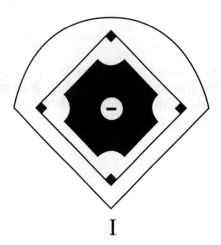

I

In the key of C major, the I chord (said like "one," not "eye") is the "home base" chord. Also known as the tonic, the I chord gives us a sense of stability as if not much is happening, like a baseball game that hasn't begun yet.

Play and hold a C chord:

I chord = stable

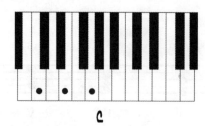

Just consider its sound for a moment. It feels stable like it doesn't need to move. It seems to say to us, "I may just sit here for a while or I may move onto a new chord." It also implicitly suggests to our ear that "we be in the key of C."

70

Third Base - The V7 Chord

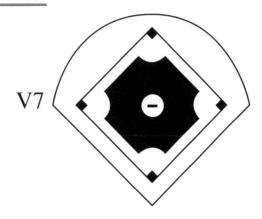

Working backwards from home base, we come to third base - the last location a baseball player occupies before heading home to score. Consider the tension the runner on third base feels as he watches the pitcher and batter, itching to head home.

Musically, this is the dwelling place of the V7 (say it like "five-seven") chord. In the key of C major, the V7 chord is a G7. Also known as a dominant seven chord, the V7 chord sounds like it wants to move onward to the next chord which is most often the I chord (C).

Play and hold the V7 chord.

V7 chord = restless

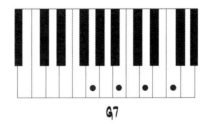

Observe how it feels unresolved, like a player on third base itching to go home.

Let this really sink in by listening to and comparing the I and V7 chords. Play these chords back and forth a couple of times considering how their sound suggest restlessness and stability.

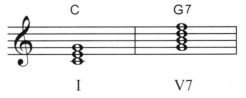

Now, play it one more time and just let the V7 chord hang....

To most people, this produces a bit of tension that feels slightly uncomfortable like it's not finished.

Home Run - The V7 - I Cadence

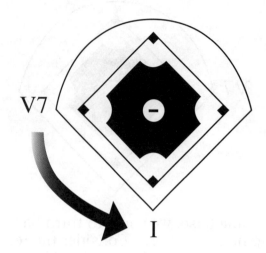

The batter hit it out of the park! The runner crosses home plate! The audience relaxes. People enjoy another bite of their hot dogs. That's the sound of a V7 chord moving to a I chord.

Play I - V7 - I (or C - G7 - C):

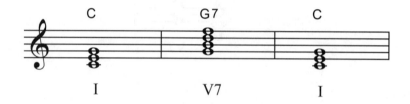

Can you hear how it resolves (releases) to sound more finished?

A short sequence of chords that move from tension to release like this is called a cadence. V7 - I is the most common cadence. The relationship between these chords is heard more clearly when they are played in their most common inversions:

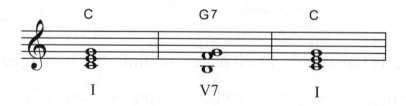

In summary, when we hear the V7 chord, our ear expects it to resolve to the I chord. That's the function of the V7 chord - to create an expectation that the I chord will follow.

> *Scott:* Does that mean that V7 chords are always followed by I chords?
>
> *Bradley:* Often, but not always...V7 - I is just a very strong tendency worth noting and being able to recognize when you hear it.

Throughout the history of Western music, composers and musicians have made use of the tendency of V7 "away" chords to point to I "home" chords. In fact, V7 - I is used so frequently in classical music that old-timers called it the authentic cadence, as if other cadences were somehow not genuine.

Scott: *What about the other principal chord? What's the function of the IV chord?*

Bradley: *The IV chord is like an "on the way" chord.*

Second Base - The IV Chord

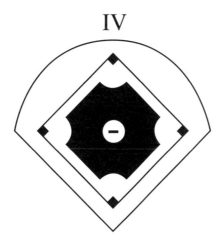

Working backwards again, the runner on 2nd base (IV chord) is in-between the action. For the audience, this player is interesting but not quite as engaging as the runner on 3rd base who is homeward bound. The function of the IV chord is to move the music along and "prepare" our ear for the V7 chord. You usually find a IV chord somewhere between the I and V7.

If we listen to the following chord progression, we can imagine a little story as a metaphor for how the chords function. Play it slowly to see if you think it fits:

The music is up to bat at home plate (I). It's a hit, it moves away from home to second base (IV). It continues to third base (V7), where it aches to move on. It returns home (I).

Scott: *What about first base?*

Bradley: *Let's skip it for now. We'll explore that one in the turnarounds section coming up.*

Here's a summary of principal chord functions:
    I = stable
    IV = moves forward, tends to point toward V7
    V7 = restless, usually resolves to I

Scott: *How is all this useful in real life piano playing?*

Bradley: *Understanding how chords function helps when you're trying to figure out the chords to a song. It's also essential to creating satisfying introductions, turnarounds and endings as we shall see.*

CHAPTER 8 – INTROS, TURNAROUNDS AND ENDINGS

Scott: *One of the things that distinguish professional pianists from the rest of us is the ability to transition. They know how to move from silence into the beginning of a song with a nice introduction. They know how to tie together repeating choruses within a song and they know how to wrap it up with an appropriate ending. This chapter will give you insights into some of the techniques they use.*

Scott: *How do you start a song?*

Bradley: *With a V7 chord.*

Scott: *How do you repeat a song?*

Bradley: *With a V7 chord plus a few others.*

Scott: *How do you end a song?*

Bradley: *With a I chord.*

Scott: *Is this going to be another chapter about music theory?*

Bradley: *Nope. Here's where we put our knowledge to use.*

Introductions

First, a quick review in case time has passed between this and the preceding chapter:

Chord functions:
    I = stable
    IV = moves forward, tends to point toward V7
    V7 = restless, usually resolves to I

The Master of Ceremonies V7 Chord

Most songs begin on a I chord. For example, *Twinkle, Twinkle Little Star* is in the key of C major and the first chord is a C chord.

Introductions happen before the song. They represent extra music that has been tagged onto the beginning before the melody actually starts.

Since a V7 chord is the most likely chord to precede a I chord, simply playing a G7 before launching into the melody effectively prepares our ear for the first chord. The V7 chord is like a master of ceremonies whose job is to build expectation by saying "and now ladies and gentlemen (drum roll please)..."

Time Stretch

Stretching out the time in an intro before the steady beat of a tune increases the sense of expectation. In the example above, the "bird's eye" symbols above and below the G7 are fermatas. They indicate that the G7 chord is to be held longer than written according to your taste.

Passing Note Bass

We can insert a snippet of a passing note bass between the V7 chord and the melody. You'll recognize this familiar lead-in:

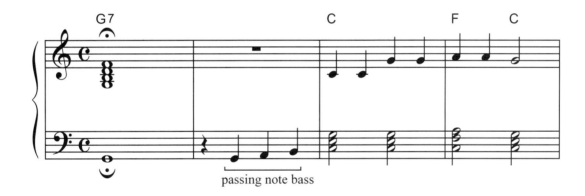

Hand Over Hand

You can stretch out the G7 even further by playing a broken chord pattern hand-over-hand moving up the keyboard. It looks harder on paper than it is to play. Just keep playing the notes in a G7 chord (G, B, D, F - G, B, D, F) while alternating hands.

By the way, that 8va with the dashed lines over those five notes tells you to play them one octave higher than written. So, every time you play the G7 with a different hand, you are jumping up to the next octave. It's a good idea to really hang on to that high note G with your sustain pedal so the listener is aching for the song to start. (This also gives you a moment to get your hands in position to begin the melody.)

Scott: *This is a great one with which to impress your friends. Liberace, here we come!*

Bradley: *Agreed. People love to see hands flying one over the other.*

If you want to really get fancy, you can play each group twice, first with the right-hand and then with the left. The effect is dazzling if you play it fast.

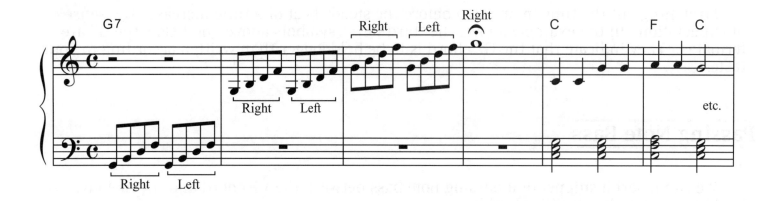

Last Few Measures

A common introduction that is especially useful for singalongs is to play the last few measures of the song. Hearing a little excerpt of the tune reminds the singers how it goes and helps them find the key and tempo. Here are the last few measures of *When the Saints Go Marching In*:

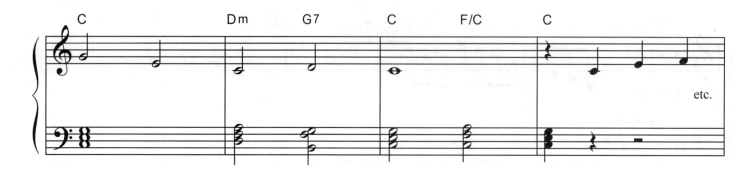

Send in a Substitution

By the time we get to the last chord, everyone is ready to chime in, or at least settle back and enjoy an old favorite. However, we can further enhance this introduction by playing a V7 (G7) near the end in place of the chords that are written:

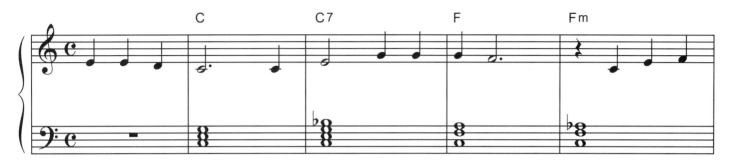

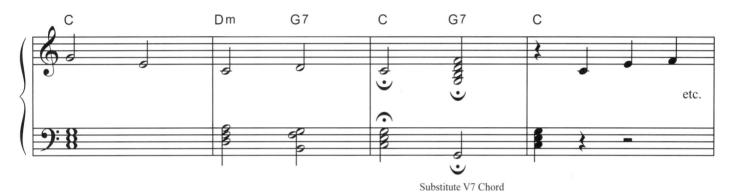

Substitute V7 Chord

Replacing one chord with another is called chord substitution. Since a V7 (G7) chord normally precedes a I (C) chord, this substitution lets us know the song is about to begin.

Combinations

It's often a good idea to combine various approaches. For example, here's the same introduction except that the substitute V7 chord uses the hand-over-hand technique:

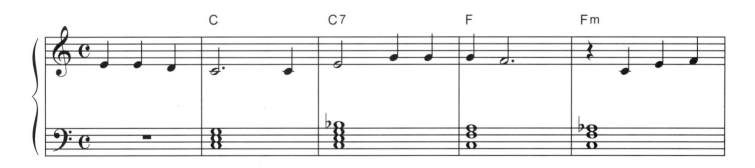

Scott: *Now, that's an introduction! How do we find out more about introductions?*

Bradley: *I recommend listening to recordings and experimenting with variations of your own. Once you understand the principles, it's easier to understand what you are hearing.*

Turnarounds

Professional pianists often insert a little unwritten chord progression right before a song repeats called a turnaround. The effect is to cause the music to wind up on itself and shoot back to the top.

Scott: *Sounds like a nice trick but why is it necessary?*

Bradley: *Turnarounds cover dead spots between choruses (repeats) of a song.*

We mentioned earlier that most songs begin on a I chord. It not so much a rule as it is a tendency. However, almost every song ever written ends on a I chord. Except for rare endings that are deliberately enigmatic, you can pretty much count on the last chord of any song being a I chord. Now, if your song both begins and ends on the same chord, there's going to be a static point between the end of the first time through and the beginning of the repeat.

For example, *She'll Be Comin' 'Round the Mountain* begins and ends on a I chord. The version we have been using is in G major, so in this key, the I chord is a G chord. Here are the last few measures as written:

She'll Be Comin' 'Round the Mountain

Folk Song

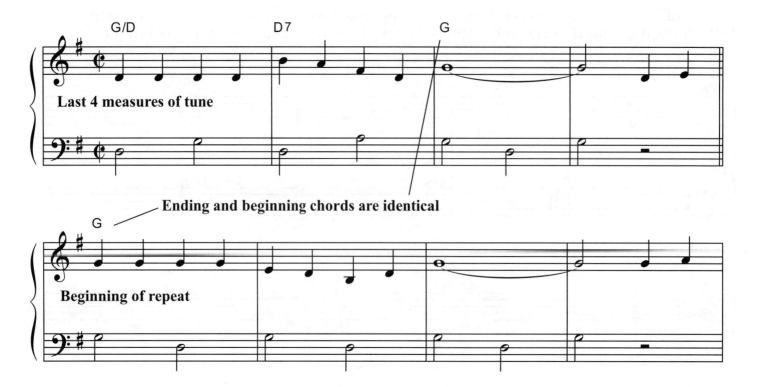

The G chord at the end sounds as if the song has come to an end. In fact, the only clue that the song will continue are the last two pickup notes (D, E) in the right-hand.

78

Notice that if we repeat this tune, the ending and beginning chords are identical. They are both G chords. This redundancy makes the song harmonically stagnant if you play it more than one time through.

Scott: *What a juicy piece of jargon. Next time someone asks how I'm doing, I'm going to reply I'm feeling "harmonically stagnant" and watch their eyebrows furl.*

Bradley: *How about chordal monotony? Call it what you will, the problem is too darn many measures of the same chord.*

Substitute V7 Chord (Again)

To break up the monotony, we can substitute a V7 chord near the end just like we did in the introduction to *When the Saints Go Marching In* earlier. *She'll Be Comin' 'Round the Mountain* is in G major. The 5th note of the G major scale is the note D so the V7 chord in this key is D7. Just insert a D7 chord into the last measure of the song, throw in a few passing notes along the way you'll be sending us 'round the mountain again with a first class turnaround:

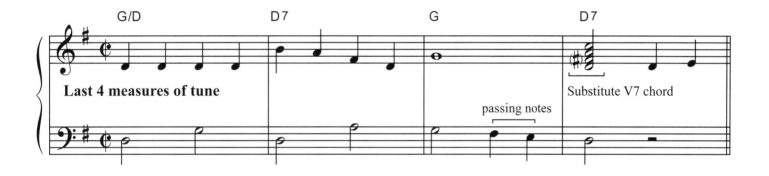

Can you hear how that D7 sends us back home for the start of the repeat? That's what a turnaround does. We can really rev up the anticipation by adding a few chords. First, let's learn the chords.

79

The ii7 Chord

In the key of G major, the second note of the scale is the note A. By stacking thirds on this note, you end up with an A minor chord:

(Remember that the Roman numeral uses lower case to indicate minor.)

We can add a 7 to this chord by stacking on another 3rd. This one is in root position:

In a moment, we'll use the inversion below of the same chord to make it easier to play with other chords.

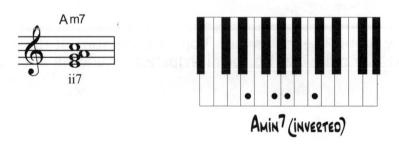

Second Base Substitution

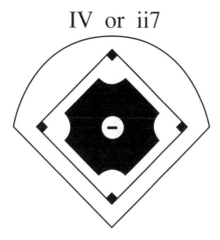

Back to our baseball diamond analogy! Like a baseball player coming out of the dugout to replace a tired teammate, the ii7 chord is often used as a substitute for the IV chord. It's easy to see why. In the key of G major, the IV is the chord C made up of the notes (C, E, G):

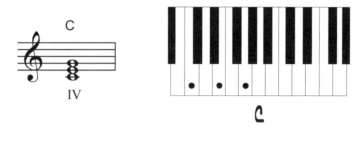

C chord = (C, E, G)

The Am7 contains all of the notes of the C chord within it (A, and then C, E, G).

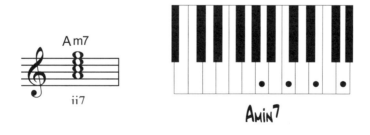

Am7 chord = (A, C, E, G)

Since they overlap so much, they can often be interchanged. The ii7 and the IV chord also function in the same way, which is to point to the V7 chord. In fact, the ii7 and IV chords are the most common chords to precede a V7 chord.

First Base - The vi Chord

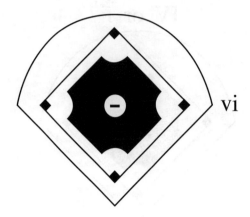

One more chord and we'll be ready to construct an all time favorite turnaround. In the key of G major, the sixth note of the scale is the note E. By stacking thirds on this note, you end up with an E minor chord:

Like a first base runner who hopes to make it home but is not sure if it will happen, the function of the vi chord is uncertain. It has a tendency to precede the ii7 (or IV) chord but it's not a given.

The Classic Turnaround

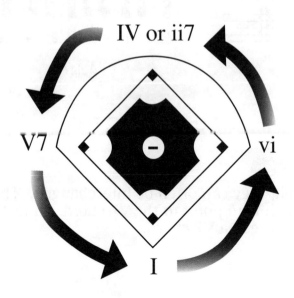

Musicians often set up repeats by substituting the following chords for the monotonous I chord in the last two measures of songs. You've heard it a million times. Now you can play it:

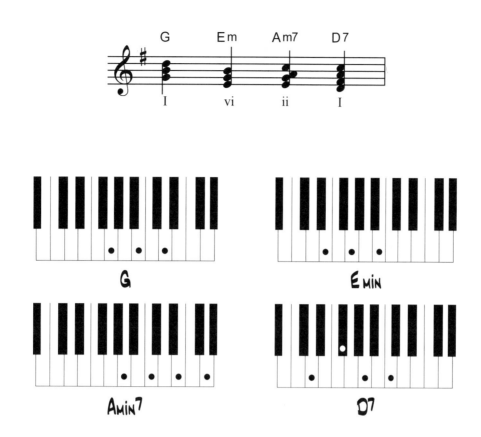

Here's the same turnaround in context with the chords in the left-hand:

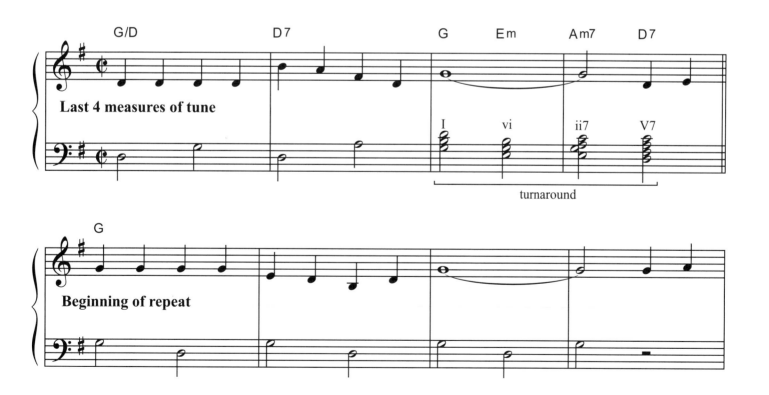

Scott: That sounds great. Why does that work so well?

Bradley: Each chord prepares our ear for the next chord.

I ⇒ vi ⇒ ii7 ⇒ V7

They just sound "right" in that order.

Scott: Does that mean that these four chords are always found in this order?

Bradley: No, but you do see and hear this progression often.

Scott: Remind us why we think about chords in terms of Roman numerals whether than just actual chords like D7.

Bradley: The beauty of understanding chord progressions such as this turnaround in the abstract is that you can transpose it to other keys. Nice segue, huh?

Transposing Turnarounds

Suppose you wanted to use the classic turnaround in another key. For example, *When the Saints Go Marching In* in C major. We know the classic turnaround in G major from *Comin' 'Round the Mountain* is as follows:

G Major Turnaround:

Chord Symbol:	G	Em	Am7	D7
Scale Position:	I	vi	ii7	V7

In the key of C major, the chords are different but the relationship remains the same:

C Major Turnaround:

Chord Symbol:	C	Am	Dm7	G7
Scale Position:	I	vi	ii7	V7

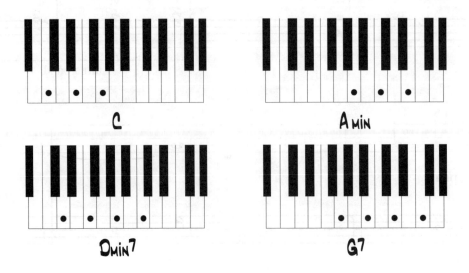

Here then, is the same classic turnaround in C major for *When the Saints Go Marching In*.

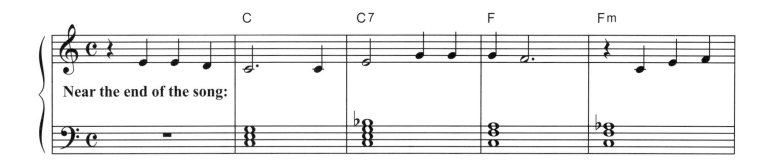

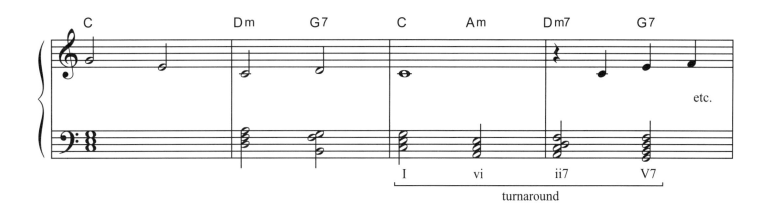

Endings

> *Scott: How do you end a song?*
>
> *Bradley: Home sweet home...point the way by leading up to it.*

As we've discussed, songs end on I chords. A song in C major ends on a C chord. That's a given so it's actually not the last chord that makes a good ending. Rather, it's the chords leading up to the last chords that create a satisfying finish.

In the last chapter, we looked at cadences - short chord sequences that move from tension to release. The authentic cadence (V7 - I) is the most often used ending.

Authentic Cadence:

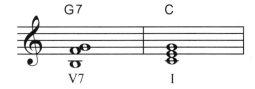

When you get to the end of a song, you can let the listener know you're finished by tossing in a V7 before the final I chord.

85

For example, *Twinkle, Twinkle Little Star* already has an authentic cadence built in:

Here it is on *Saints*:

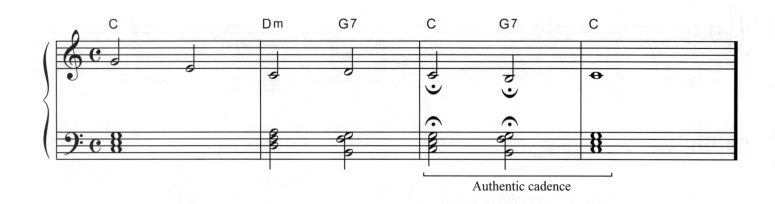

If you want to be dramatic, you can repeat the authentic cadence over and over in a variety of rhythms.   This was a favorite trick of the old masters.

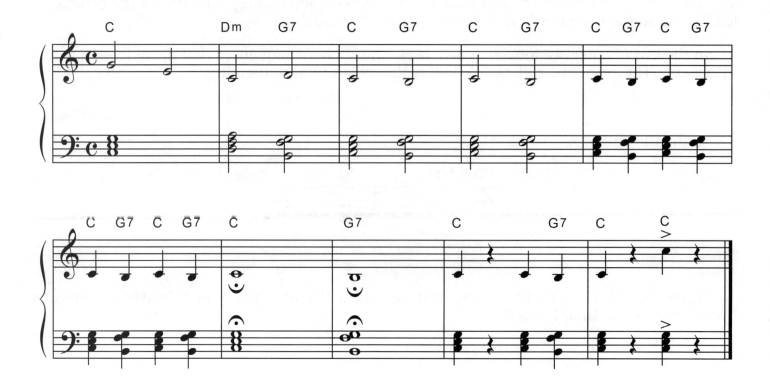

86

The masters used the authentic cadence, but so has every cheesy musician you've ever heard:

Plagal Cadence - Amen!

Another popular ending is the IV - I or plagal cadence. Here it is in the key of G major where IV is a C chord and I is a G chord:

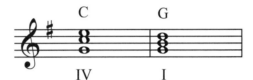

This is sometimes called the "amen" cadence since you often hear it at the end of gospel songs and hymns.

A good trick is to play the IV over the home note of the key to help push it home. In the key of G major, play the C chord in your right hand over the note G in your left hand.

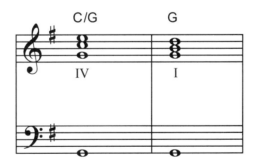

Here's an ending you'll recognize that places a little lick over the plagal cadence:

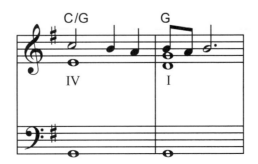

A variation of this ending involves passing chords moving down from IV (C) to I (G).

To put it in context, here's the plagal cadence on the last four measures of *Amazing Grace*:

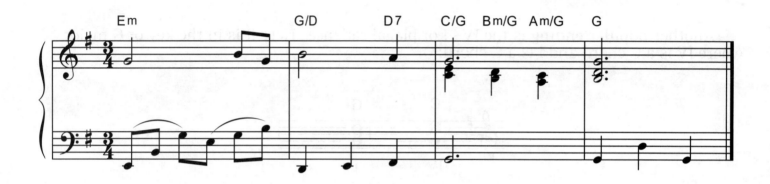

Scott: That's a gospel sound we all recognize. What are some other endings associated with specific styles?

Bradley: The best thing to do is listen to recordings and figure out your favorites by ear, but here are a few to get started.

Rock Whole Step Ending

A popular rock style ending is to move from the final chord down to the chord a whole step (2 half steps) below and then back again. It's like a guitar player sliding the chord down the neck and back:

88

A variation of this ending is to insert the chord that lies 1/2 step below the final chord on your way back. Again, it's like a guitar player sliding the same chord up fret by fret:

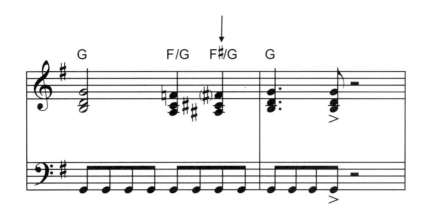

You can keep the bass on the home note G or move it along with the chords as in this little example:

Scott: *Did you make that one up? Wasn't that a rock ending to* Comin' Round The Mountain?

Bradley: *Okay, so it may not ever make the hit parade, but you get the idea. Boy, tough crowd...*

Jazz Cadence - The Sideslip

A common jazz ending is like the rock cadence but it moves up instead of down. After playing the final chord, simply slide up a half step and back:

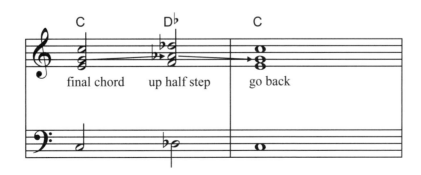

It works in any inversion. Just move your chord position up and back.

It's a nice to effect to hang on to the second to last chord for a little suspense or even shake it (tremolo) as in this example that ends *When the Saints Go Marching In*:

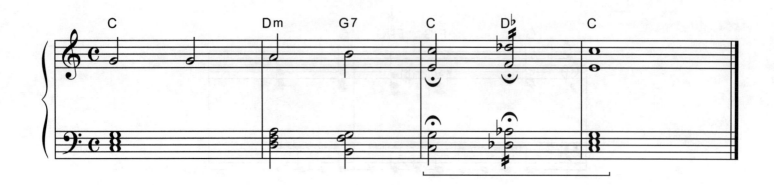

Many styles have specific introductions, turnarounds and endings associated with them that are beyond the reach of this book. The licks and rhythms will vary, but the principles remain the same. Now that you understand chord function, turnarounds and common cadences, you'll have an easier time figuring them out by ear.

Remember music is an aural art, not a written one. Listening and imitating is not only NOT cheating, it is the authentic way to learn a lot of the tehniques used in our style of non-classical playing. Don't feel funny "hunting and pecking" and experimenting with intros, turnarounds, and endings. It's the way most pros learned them…

CHAPTER 9 – PUTTING IT ALL TOGETHER

Scott: *This book has presented a lot of information about going further with a lead sheet. If you've read this far and played through the examples, you've learned plenty. This chapter offers tips on putting your knowledge together to create satisfying arrangements of songs you enjoy playing. It also includes practical tips on playing by ear.*

Scott: *We've learned a lot of tips and tricks of the trade in this book. Now, how do we sit down and really play a song?*

Bradley: *First, take time to work out the various parts of a song. Then put it all together.*

Whether using music notation, improvisation or playing from memory, the solo pianist builds an arrangement step by step. Like a magnificent building, each part of the structure is basic but the effect of all the parts working together impresses us.

Here are the steps to building your unique version of song:

    1. Pick a song
    2. Find a source
    3. Create a skeletal version
    4. Pick a style
    5. Work out the mechanics
    6. Add in the extras
    7. Put it all together

Let's take a closer look at these steps.

1. Pick a song

What do you want to play?

Believe it or not, plenty of musicians have a hard time answering this one. They like music, but can't decide which song they should buckle down and learn. Here are some considerations that, although obvious, are not often thought about:

    a) What kind of music do you like?
    b) Who are your most likely listeners?
    c) Where would you like to play? Answering this question will help you focus on specific genres. Here's a chart to set you thinking:

Where to play:	What to play:
Holiday office party	Perhaps some carols are in order
Singalongs	Camp songs and folk melodies
Church	Hymns and spirituals
On a date	Love songs
For personal pleasure	Pick a decade - 60s, 70s, 80s...
Lounge setting	Tin pan alley songs, Broadway
For kids	Children's songs and movie themes

2. Find a source

a) Fake Books - A fake book is a collection of songs in lead sheet form with only the melody and chord symbols. Professional musicians use them to "fake" (improvise) arrangements to songs. You can use them to gather songs and create your own arrangements from scratch. All of the genres in the previous chart and many more are available in published fake books.

b) Written arrangements - Publishers offer arrangements of popular songs such as current hits or movie themes in single sheets for solo piano. Sometimes these written arrangements are very well put together and sometimes they are cheesy. Whatever the case, they are never the "definitive" version. They only represent one arranger's attempt to make a song playable by most intermediate pianists. Suppose you are not a good enough reader to play the arrangement. These sheets are still valuable because most of them have chord symbols and a melody or vocal line that stands out from the accompaniment. In other words, the parts that make up a lead sheet (the melody line a chord symbols) are embedded in the full arrangement. That's what you want. Chords and melody are the essence of a tune. The rest is somebody else's filler with which you have three choices:

1. Play what is written.
2. Use some of what is written such as specific left hand patterns to add to your bag of tricks.
3. Put together your own version using the chords and melody as raw material.

The point is that you don't have to feel restricted by what's on the page as if some sort of music police officer is going to nab you if you play something else.

Scott: *What if it's a song you know well enough to sing but you can't find it in sheet music form?*

Bradley: *You work it out by ear.*

Scott: *I thought that was only for people who have perfect pitch.*

Bradley: *Anyone who can sing a tune can work it out on the keyboard. But there are some specific steps you can take to increase your success.*

c) Play by Ear - You already know loads of simple, classic melodies that can be harmonized with the three principal chords outlined in the first chapter of this book. You don't have to be a musical genius to do it. Just follow these steps:

1. *Work it out in the key of C* - Everything is easier in C. You can always transpose it later. Begin by playing the principal chords in the key of C to get the sound of the key squarely in your head.
2. *Find the home note* - Sing the song in the key of C to determine the "home" (tonic) note, which is the same as the key of the song. Work backwards. The last note of a melody is nearly always the tonic. Make sure this is the note C.
3. *Find the first note* - A lot of people get into trouble by assuming the first note of the song is the home note but that's not always the case. With the sound of the key still in your head, play up a C scale until you find the first note.
4. *Work out the melody* - Get the melody down cold in just your right hand before you think about chords.
5. *Match the Chords* - Look for chord tones in the melody. In the key of C, the principal chords are C (I) with the notes (C, E, G), F (IV) with the notes (F, A, C) and G7 (V7) with the notes (G, B, D, F).

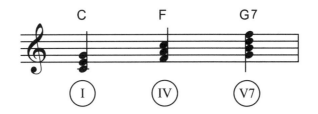

When the notes in a melody match the notes in one of these chords, there's a good chance that chord will fit.

Let's see how this works in practice:

Suppose you are working out the melody to *On Top of Old Smoky* by ear but you don't know the chords. You've already taken the preliminary steps of singing through it so you realize that the song begins and ends on the note C. Now you are ready to harmonize it.

Look at the first four notes in the melody:

The opening notes are C, E, and G. These are the same notes that make up a C chord. With a 100% match between the melody notes and chord tones, you can bet the C chord will fit here.

Moving on, the next measure only has the note C. With just this one note, there are two possible chords that will fit since the note C is in the C chord (C, E, G) as well as the F chord (F, A, C):

Which one is it? Find out by trying both. What does your ear tell you? You can also look a bit further. If we assume that the chord in question encompasses two measures, we can consider both the notes C and A:

Only the F chord contains both notes C and A. So you try it out to see if it fits:

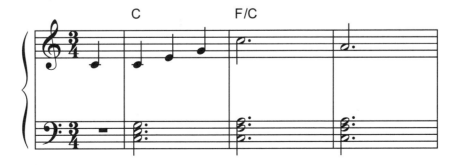

It does! And on it goes until you've harmonized the whole song.

93

Challenge:
See if you can play these songs "by ear" with no music or lead sheet. All of them use principal chords exclusively. After you've figured out the melody in your right hand, see if you can determine which left hand principal chords match up.

<u>Songs that use just the C chord:</u>
Frere Jacque also known as Are You Sleeping Brother John? (starts on C)
Row, Row, Row Your Boat (starts on C)

<u>Songs that use the chords C and G7:</u>
Mary Had A Little Lamb (starts on E)
London Bridge is Falling Down (starts on G)

<u>Songs that use C, F, and G7:</u>
Joy to the World (starts on high C)
Red River Valley (starts on G)

3. Creating a skeletal version

The next step to building a unique version of a song is to establish the basics:

a) Make sure you know and can play the melody in your right hand.
b) Find inversions of the chords that are easy to play so your left hand isn't jumping all around the keyboard.
c) Position your hands. Sometimes you have to move your right hand up an octave or your left hand down an octave so your hands don't overlap.

4. Pick a style

There are many common basslines and left hand patterns that are associated with specific genres such as jazz or latin that are beyond the scope of this book. However, you can pick an overall feel using adjectives such as "bouncy" or "smoothly connected." Ask yourself what suits this particular song. How is it usually played?

5. Work out the mechanics

This is really the nitty gritty of putting together a song where you determine how to combine melody, harmony and bassline. Here's a list of some of the possibilities we explored in this book.

a) Add motion with broken chord patterns such as Alberti Bass.
b) Suggest a bassline by varying the left chord inversions.
c) Use passing notes to enhance that bassline.
d) Employ an EZ Bass that focuses on roots and 5ths.
e) Play the chords in your right hand with your pinky on the melody.
f) Create an open/closed left hand broken chord pattern.
g) Use faux stride that mixes roots and 5ths with chords.

Here are the considerations in making a choice:

a) Which approach seems possible within your current technical ability? This is a practical but important matter. Sometimes, student musicians strive to make things more complex in the belief that it will be better, when listeners actually appreciate a clear and simple approach that is played well.

b) Which approach seems to suit the song? Some songs beg for a particular treatment. For example, the classical sound of *Twinkle, Twinkle Little Star* makes it a good candidate for the Alberti Bass. Of course, it's always fun to go beyond expectations and find some other way to perform a classic, which leads to the next consideration.

c) Which approach will support the style or personal take on the song that you wish to convey? For example, the EZ Bass tends to be more bouncy than smoother broken chords. Perhaps, a normally peppy song would sound more interesting if it were played slower or vice versa.

6. Add in the extras

a) Intro - Pick an introduction that suits the overall feel you developed in the previous step. Decide whether you will play the last few measures or if a simple V7 chord will suffice.

b) Turnaround - Figure out how to set the song up so it will repeat more than once. Will you use the classic I - vi - ii7 - V7 progression, substitute a V7 chord or perhaps the song doesn't need a turnaround?

c) Ending - Too many musicians just sort of stop at the end of the song. Take the time to work out a snazzy finish, perhaps using one of the cadences we explored in this book.

7. Put it all together

Like a building with a basement, lobby, separate floors and a roof, songs have form. Determine the order of the various parts of your song and keep it in your head like a road map as you play. There are many ways to organize the form but the following would be fairly typical:

a) Set up the song with an introduction

b) Play the melody in a fairly straightforward manner

c) Repeat the melody in an embellished fashion

d) Improvise over the song's chord progression - this can be the whole song or just the first half

e) Repeat the melody in some enhanced way - this can be the whole song or the remaining half after your improvisation

f) Tag it with an ending

> *Scott:*   *Can you give us an example where it all comes together?*
>
> *Bradley:*   *You bet!*

The written example on the next page uses several of the techniques we explored in this book. It represents only one of many possible ways that a song could be turned into an arrangement. There is no one right or wrong way to do it. Your arrangement of this tune would sound different than this because it would be yours!

Amazing Grace

Setting by Bradley Sowash

96

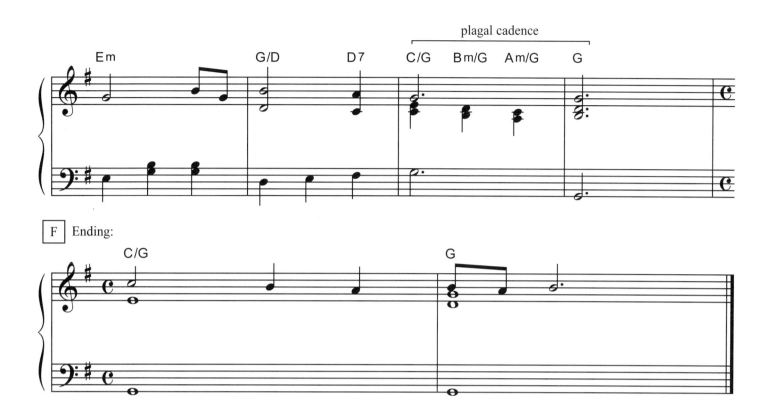

Scott: What's the last thing you should do when you've finished playing your arrangement of a song?

Bradley: Take a bow and smile!

Scott: Now, we've come to the end of this book.

Bradley: But it's really just the beginning.

Scott: Right, I encourage you, the reader, to find some songs you would like to play and make the effort to put them together using the techniques we've outlined here.

Bradley: Do it today while these ideas are still fresh in your mind.

Happy music making from both of us,

Scott Houston   and   Bradley Sowash